BOROBUDUR

Golden Tales of the Buddhas

BOROBUDUR
Golden Tales of the Buddhas

TEXT BY JOHN MIKSIC

PHOTOGRAPHS BY
MARCELLO AND ANITA TRANCHINI

PERIPLUS
EDITIONS

Published by Periplus Editions (HK) Ltd.

Distributors

Indonesia:
C.V. Java Books, P.O. Box 55 JKCP, Jakarta 10510
Singapore and Malaysia:
Berkeley Books Pte. Ltd.,
5 Little Road, #08-01 Cemtex Industrial Building,
Singapore 536983

Publisher: Eric Oey
Editors: Eric Oey and Anne Cherian
Design, photo editing and production: Peter Ivey
Illustrations: Lucille Tham

ISBN 0-945971-90-7

Printed in Indonesia

All photographs by Marcello and Anita Tranchini, except as noted:

Pages 6-7, 31, 52 by Kal Muller; pages 8-9, 40 by Luca Invernizzi
Tettoni; pages 10-11 by Rio Helmi; pages 18, 21, 29, 30 courtesy of
the Leiden University Library; page 22 courtesy of the Ethnographic
Museum, Leiden; page 28 courtesy of the Prentenkabinet, Leiden;
page 32 by Eric Oey; page 53 by Tom Ballinger;
page 67 by John Miksic.

*The publisher wishes to express special thanks to Dr. H.I.R. Hinzler of
Leiden University for her assistance in obtaining prints and
photographs from Dutch collections.*

Frontispiece: Manohara the nymph as she escapes pursuers bent on her
destruction. From the *avadana* reliefs on the first gallery (I.b11).
Pages 6-7: The silhouette of Borobudur, dominated by the towering
mass of the central stupa, hovers above the cool early morning mists
and lush foliage of central Java's Kedu Plain.
Pages 8-9: An aerial view of Borobudur seen from the north.
Numerous traces of a large pilgrimage center have been found beneath
the surface of the plain in the background.
Pages 10-11: Sunrise over the Kedu Plain, with Mt. Merapi (right) and
Mt. Merbabu (left) in the background. The view is identical to those
which would have greeted monks at the conclusion of nocturnal
meditations a thousand years ago.

Contents

Photographer's Preface

BOROBUDUR'S RELIEFS ARE LIKE A GREAT COLLAR OF precious jewels set all around the walls of the monument—even if water, atmospheric conditions and looters have damaged some of the panels. The beauty of these reliefs cannot be perceived by superficial and hasty eyes. Unfortunately, some visitors drag themselves wearily around the galleries, exhausted by the prospect of the lengthy corridors, while others, after brief attempts to rest on various levels, set off decisively for the summit to admire the view from the round terraces, ignoring altogether the real beauty of the monument.

In ancient times the pilgrim to Borobudur circumambulated the narrow corridors on each level in slow succession. Keeping the main wall of the monument always to his right, meditating and praying, he traced a slow but spiritual progress to the summit. Proceeding upward in this fashion, he achieved an ever purer state of mind, progressively detaching himself from the miseries of the world. The spaces created by Borobudur's architects reinforce this process, for the lower levels are labyrinthine and mysterious, while the higher ones gradually open and fill with life. When at last the pilgrim reaches the end of the mystic path, physically tired but fresh and vibrant in spirit, he has finally gained his objective: he is alone, close to Buddha and to Heaven.

The modern-day pilgrim, attracted by the art of the monument, must be prepared to trace a similar route. Slowly and patiently treading in the footsteps of the faithful, allowing the eye to grow accustomed to the condition of the carved stone panels, he thus discovers one of the greatest artistic creations in this world.

Even the most simple work of art needs the proper setting, the proper moment and the proper state of mind in order to be appreciated. This combination is supremely well-achieved at Borobudur, which stands imposingly alone in the isolated Kedu Valley. Gazing at the delicate figures and harmonious compositions, progressing through the silent and narrow corridors between the stones and the sky, the modern pilgrim is filled with a sense of divinity and the belief that he, too, is approaching Buddha's paradise.

The sculptors of Borobudur created a series of incomparable images, giving each figure a delicate and meek demeanor which is the essence of Buddhism. Over the centuries, the hot sun of the tropics seems to have added to the work of the artisans, painting its own royal yellow onto the soft volcanic stone. The predominant color is an antique, serene and faded gold which bestows an even more magical charm—as if someone had gently applied gold powder to the faces and bodies of these immobile figures. The stones whose good fortune it is to face the sunset, especially, have acquired this ultimate wonder.

To properly convey their beauty, the photographer has to develop a particularly intimate relationship with the sculptures. He must wait patiently for the right sunbeam to illuminate a sweet face, or wander anxiously in search of a particular figure, and will often feel a surge of excitement upon returning to a familiar stone. Above all, he experiences the joy of discovering not only the splendor of the sculptures' forms, but the breath of their soul—the soul of ancient Indonesia which still shines through thousands of charming and smiling eyes. The photographer and the sculpture face to face—one alive, the other still and fixed for centuries but equally rich with life. The one has lips that speak, the other lips that seem to whisper distant sounds.

The photographer is indeed fortunate. Photographing Borobudur has given me a keen sense of acquiring the infinite beauty of the masterpiece—of capturing it from the walls and carrying it home.

My intention here is not to strive for completeness. This book will have served its purpose if a substantial sampling of the most beautiful and significant bas-reliefs are made available to a wider public. My hope is that this may further stimulate and aid the studies of those who visit Borobudur, and keep alive the recollections of those who have toiled up its well-worn steps.

Marcello Tranchini

Author's Preface

Borobudur was intended to foster a form of spiritual education in an atmosphere of rational serenity, free from the distortions of human emotion. Even the faces of sinners shown on the hidden foot undergoing various punishments in hell are calm, if not smiling. The Javanese of today, although Muslims, still prize a state of unwavering emotional detachment, and although one cannot be certain, it is likely that the same ideal was sought and to a great extent attained in ancient Java when Borobudur was built—how else to explain the consistent emotional tone sustained over hundreds of meters of reliefs carved by scores of different craftsmen?

Ironically, Borobudur's effect on modern scholars has been almost the opposite of what its designers intended. Multitudes of conflicting theories have been proposed to explain the monument's name, design and ultimate meaning. While some of the disputes regarding the symbolism of Borobudur's various parts have been resolved, the meaning of the monument as a whole remains a mystery.

Progress in the disciplines of ancient Javanese history and archaeology has been slow but constant. New archaeological sites and inscriptions are excavated each year, and with the unearthing of each new tool, weapon and piece of jewelry, we learn a bit more about ancient Javanese economy and society. This new data joins a dialogue with information preserved in the form of Borobudur and other ancient monuments. The advances thus obtained in various fields interact with one another in a way that may be compared to the enormous net of jewels covering the palace of Indra, King of the Gods—in which each jewel reflects rays of light from all the others.

A monument such as Borobudur is different from ordinary buildings because its main purpose is symbolic. Monuments are not good at expressing complex or subtle ideas, yet they are one of the most powerful means at man's disposal to present simple messages to a great number of people. Most monuments present striking silhouettes which may be seen from a great distance and excite strong feelings of wonder, respect or determination. The ancient Javanese had such monuments also—the Siva complex at Prambanan is a prime example.

Borobudur's builders eschewed such a purpose, wanting instead to engage the mind. Borobudur's message is too complex to state with a simple shape, and the monument does not proclaim itself loudly. Instead it reposes gently, its outline quietly hinting at great power lying beneath the surface.

Borobudur is not a monument at all in this sense, but a tool for instilling a particular philosophy, for presenting a doctrine about no less complex a subject than the very meaning of existence. Borobudur's builders could have fulfilled the same goal by writing a dry series of lectures. Instead they created a work of art with immense capacity to give pleasure to people with little or no interest in Buddhism. Its power to affect people from times and places so distant from its builders marks it as a masterpiece of human culture.

This book is intended to enhance the enjoyment which one obtains from Borobudur and its reliefs, by describing what is known of the ancient Javanese who built it and of the symbols which they employed to express their conception of man's place in the universe.

In addition to the written sources I have consulted, I am deeply grateful to four brilliant scholars who have shared their ideas with me in conversation: J.G. de Casparis, J. Dumarçay, J. Fontein, and R. Soekmono. Their influence permeates each page of this book. I would also like to express my gratitude to Kwa Chong Guan who helped me gain access to sources on Buddhism difficult to obtain in Singapore.

This book is dedicated to my friends and colleagues in the Department of Archaeology, Gajah Mada University, Yogyakarta, among whom I spent six of the happiest years of my life.

John Miksic

PART I

History and Archaeology

THE FIRST RECORDED VISITOR TO BORObudur was neither a monk nor a scholar. He was a rebel. In 1709 or 1710 Ki Mas Dana rose against the ruler of central Java but was defeated. A Javanese chronicle states that "Many rebels died, whereupon Ki Mas Dana fled to the mountain Bara-Budur. Prince Pringga-Laya and his troops pursued him. They surrounded the mountain, captured Ki Mas Dana, and sent him to Kartasura to be executed by the king."[1]

The next documented visitor to the monument was a crown prince, but his fate was no happier than Ki Mas Dana's. In 1758 the heir apparent of Yogyakarta defied a prophecy that royalty who visited the "mountain of the thousand statues" would die. The prince, who had a reputation for rebellious and dissolute behavior, wanted to see the famous image of a "warrior in a cage." When he showed no sign of returning to court, the king sent men to bring his son back dead or alive. The prince was captured, but vomited blood and died.[2]

By 1700 the Javanese seem to have forgotten that Borobudur had been constructed by their own ancestors. To them the name only meant a hill with a large collection of sculpture. They did not even dignify the site by calling it a *candi*, a word which the Javanese use for ruins of the pre-Islamic era. Perhaps they regarded it merely as a natural mound where their ancestors had erected statues, depicting whom they did not know. Borobudur at this time was but a somewhat ill-omened curiosity.

Borobudur Reawakens Fortune was kinder to nineteenth century visitors. Lieutenant-Governor Thomas Stamford Raffles was probably sitting in a mansion in Semarang on Java's north coast when he was told of a great ruined temple lying deep in the island's interior. Raffles was the first colonial ruler to take an interest in Javanese antiquities. A military surveyor by the name of Colin MacKenzie had already informed him of the existence of Hindu remains beside the road east of Yogyakarta. MacKenzie had spent eleven years in India and was surprised and excited to discover statues of familiar gods in this remote island where the people in his time were almost all Muslims.

Raffles had earlier formed a team under MacKenzie to survey Java and record its monuments. He also encouraged local people to bring him antiquities. Perhaps such a person came to Semarang in January of 1814 to show Raffles a bronze statue or gold coin, stayed for a while and mentioned to him that a vast monument lay in ruins in the Kedu Plain west of Yogyakarta.

MacKenzie had by this time returned to India, so to investigate the report Raffles dispatched H. C. Cornelius, a Dutch engineer who had worked closely with MacKenzie. The Javanese led Cornelius to a huge ruin so long neglected that it took 200 men a month and a half to cut and burn vegetation around it, and to remove dirt cloaking the stones to reveal the outline of the monument.

Cornelius had many drawings made—39 of which survive[3]—and submitted a report to Raffles which has never been published. It is a surprisingly matter-of-fact account of one of the nineteenth century's greatest archaeological discoveries. Although it contains few details of what he actually saw, the report is an important historical document, for it is the earliest description we have of the largest Buddhist sanctuary ever built.

Overleaf: *A lithograph by C.W. Mieling, published in 1873 but based on a sketch made by F.C. Wilsen in 1849. This is one of the most detailed early images of Borobudur. The large opening in the central stupa which several early visitors mention can be clearly seen.*

Opposite: *The very first published view of Borobudur, which appeared in the second edition of Raffles' monumental work,* The History of Java. *Based on a sketch by Cornelius, it depicts large trees growing upon the monument which do not, however, obscure the main outline of the structure.*

Borobudur as sketched by H.N. Sieburgh in 1838 from a point on Dagi Hill, 500 meters northwest of the monument. In the left foreground is a guardian statue (dvarapala) given to King Chulalongkorn in 1896, that now resides in the National Museum, Bangkok.

The discovery of such a monumental work of art in the hinterland of a remote island in Southeast Asia came as a great surprise to the outside world. This was 47 years before Henri Mouhaut called attention to the remarkable ruins of Angkor in Cambodia, and it was Borobudur's discovery that first made Europeans aware of the high level of civilization which had been attained in ancient Southeast Asia. This raised numerous questions which still persist today, more than 175 years later. How did the Buddhist faith spread to Java from its homeland in India in ancient times—a distance of over 5,000 kilometers? Why did the Javanese, rather than any of the other peoples in the vast area where Buddhism was practiced, build the largest and most elaborate Buddhist monument the world has ever known?

Buddhism in India and Beyond

Buddhism originated in India more than a thousand years before the construction of Borobudur. Siddharta Gautama[4]—later known as Buddha or "the Awakened One"—was born at the foot of the Himalaya mountains around 500 B.C. He was a member of the Sakya ethnic group; thus he is often called Sakyamuni, "Jewel of the Sakya People."[5]

Word of the new path to spiritual salvation which he disclosed was gradually spread by merchants along trade routes to many other parts of Asia. Buddhism considered merchants to be self-sacrificing people who undertook long and dangerous journeys in order to satisfy other people's needs. Merchants are depicted as heroes in the *jataka* and *avadana* stories. They felt protected by the numerous buddhas and bodhisattvas and erected many statues, inscriptions and shrines throughout Central and East Asia, from isolated oases along the Silk Route to cosmopolitan centers of culture in China and Japan. Today Buddhism and ancient traditions of Buddhist scholarship still flourish in a vast region reaching from the Himalayas to Japan, enabling us to trace Buddhism's complex development through much of this period.

From the very earliest period Buddhists have held two alternative viewpoints regarding the proper path to salvation. According to the more austere view, each person must find his own way to ultimate release from the endless cycle of rebirth. The process of spiritual advancement is long and arduous, requiring many lifetimes of sacrifice before one may escape from the rounds of reincarnation and suffering.

Within a few generations after Sakyamuni's death, some teachers began to claim that the process could be accelerated with special knowledge. People could hope to reach the state of ultimate bliss through the help of certain bodhisattvas or "enlightening beings" who had already reached the stage of perfect knowledge, but voluntarily continued to be reborn in order to protect and guide those who languished on lower levels of spiritual development. Those who believed in bodhisattvas preached that man should not seek personal salvation, for that would be selfish. Instead they taught that the greatest virtue lay in becoming a bodhisattva who sacrificed individual happiness for the welfare of others.

Two Paths to Salvation As Buddhism spread through India, bodhisattvas became increasingly popular. New scriptures appeared, giving more details about them and exploring their links with various buddhas. Some followers began to distinguish their beliefs from the simpler version of Buddhism, calling their path Mahayana, the "Greater Way" or "Vehicle." They deprecatingly termed more rigorous and individualistic teachings Hinayana, the "Lesser Vehicle." Although these two doctrines can be differentiated in theory, in practice early Buddhism combined both.

A version of Mahayana Buddhism sometimes called Esoteric Buddhism began to appear around A.D. 600. This form of Buddhism asserts that certain qualified people can shorten the path to enlightenment to a single lifetime by using appropriate techniques and devices. These ideas had an important impact on Buddhist art and architecture, as buildings came to be employed in special ceremonies to accelerate spiritual progress. These doctrines were developing rapidly at the very time when a major new trade route linking India with Java and Sumatra was opened. This new route was by sea, as opposed to the old land route to China and mainland Southeast Asia that had been in use for centuries, and many of the earliest travelers along it were Buddhist merchants and pilgrims.

During the early part of the first millennium A.D., various forms of Hinduism became influential in the lower Mekong Valley of mainland Southeast Asia. The kingdoms of this area depended more on agriculture than on trade and possessed rigid class structures, thus Hinduism's emphasis on hereditary status was highly congenial to them. Buddhism, with its more egalitarian attitude, only supplanted Hinduism as the dominant religion there in the fourteenth century, when the Theravada or "Elder Doctrine" was brought from Sri Lanka. Sumatra and Java, on the other hand, were influenced by Mahayana Buddhist ideas spread along the maritime trade routes. These precepts, with their emphasis upon special teaching devices and techniques for salvation, motivated and shaped the construction of monuments such as the temple of Borobudur.

Java and the Javanese

Ethnically as well as geographically, Java is very far removed from the homeland of Gautama Buddha. The Javanese are descended from seafarers who left the south China coast and ventured across the great oceans south and east of the Asian mainland some 6,000 years ago. Some sailed east and settled the islands of the Pacific, while others sailed south and west to Borneo, Java and beyond—even crossing the Indian Ocean to Madagascar in the first millennium A.D. Javanese sailors probably visited India even before the time of Christ, since Java is mentioned in the earliest written version (300 B.C.) of the Indian *Ramayana* epic. Graeco-Roman traders stationed in south India around A.D. 100 were impressed by large non-Indian ships bringing cargoes of pepper and spices from the east. No doubt these were Indonesians sailing from ports in Java and Sumatra.

Java is a tropical island slightly over 1000 kilometers (600 miles) long and 200 kilometers (120 miles) wide at its widest point. A chain of over 20 volcanoes, many of them quite active, runs through the center of the island. During

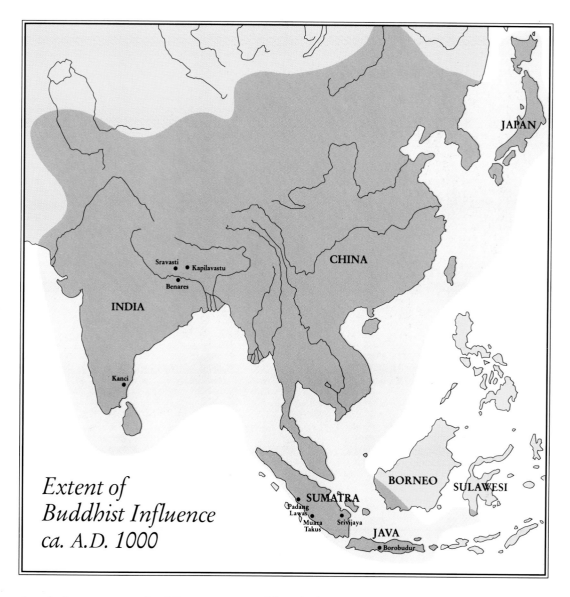

Extent of Buddhist Influence ca. A.D. 1000

the ninth century much of Java was covered by virgin jungle. Most of the island's population—probably fewer than a million people at this time—lived close to the upper courses of rivers.

Around A.D. 400 the Javanese began to carve stone statues and engrave inscriptions using motifs and alphabets from various areas of South Asia. The first kingdom known in Java, Tarumanegara, existed in the far western part of the island in the fifth century. By A.D. 700 the focus of civilization had moved to the center of the island, where the population began to construct stone temples incorporating motifs from several parts of India. In a relatively brief period of about 200 years—between

Buddhism attained the greatest extent of its influence around A.D. 1000. Though it became nearly extinct in India soon thereafter, it survives as an active religion today in many parts of Asia.

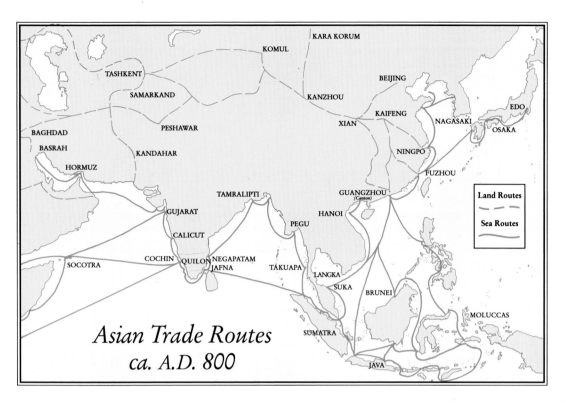

Asian Trade Routes
ca. A.D. 800

Land Routes

Sea Routes

As early as 2000 years ago, many parts of the vast Asian continent were already linked by well-established trade routes. Buddhism spread from India to mainland and insular Southeast Asia along these land and sea routes during the first millennium A.D.

we may rediscover the philosophical concepts of the Javanese which were parallel to, but not identical with, those of India.

Traders and Pilgrims

Traders along the Silk Route introduced Buddhism to China during the first centuries A.D., and the new religion soon acquired a firm foothold beside the indigenous Chinese beliefs of Taoism and Confucianism. Chinese pilgrims made the long and difficult journey to India during the first millennium A.D. to collect scriptures and visit the sites of important events in Gautama Buddha's life. Some of those who survived spent years translating precious manuscripts from Sanskrit into Chinese.

A sea link between India and China was forged several centuries later, around A.D. 400. The earliest evidence for the use of this route is found in an account of the voyage of Faxian, a Chinese monk who went to India by land to obtain scriptures and returned home on a merchant ship via Java in A.D. 414. About 10 years later a famous Buddhist teacher, Prince Gunavarman of Kashmir, spent many years in Java before proceeding to China. Both of these early pilgrims left accounts of their travels.

This new route was opened by Indonesian sailors who already had several centuries of experience in maritime trade with other parts of Southeast Asia and India. Ports in Java and Sumatra rapidly became prosperous centers of commerce and communication between India and China. This maritime connection was very important to both Chinese and Indians, particularly during the intermittent periods when the overland route was blocked by nomadic barbarians.

To Southeast Asia by Sea Buddhist pilgrims voyaged with increasing frequency through Indonesia during the seventh and eighth centuries. The records they have left tell us that Java and Sumatra were major centers of international Buddhist scholarship during this period, and provide a surprisingly vivid picture of Buddhist activities in these islands.

Yijing, a Chinese monk who visited Indonesia in the seventh century, left a particularly detailed record of Buddhist activity in various countries. In December A.D. 671 he sailed from China to the port of Srivijaya in South Sumatra, where he spent six months studying Sanskrit. Then he boarded a ship belonging to Srivijaya's ruler which took him to India, where he spent about 15 years studying and collecting Buddhist scriptures. He returned to Srivijaya around 686 and stayed there for at least five years before going home to China.

about A.D. 700 and 900—the people of central Java created an astonishing number of religious monuments. Thousand-year-old ruins lie thickly scattered over Java's interior, though many remains have disappeared in the past two centuries.

A previous generation of historians believed that ancient Java was simply a primitive land which Indian civilization penetrated by colonization, commerce, conquest and migration. They even assumed that Borobudur must have been built by Indians. After decades of research, scholars now have abundant evidence that the ancient Javanese were not mere barbarians who passively absorbed superior foreign ideas. The Javanese had already reached a high level of cultural development before the two areas came into contact. They made pottery, wove cloth, and worked bronze, iron and gold. They grew rice and other crops using a complex system of terraces and irrigation. They carved statues, built religious sanctuaries in the form of terraces faced with stone, and had an organized system of government.

The Javanese who designed and built Borobudur did not simply copy a foreign monument. Instead they blended local and Indian elements and created a new kind of sanctuary. Thus by studying how the Javanese employed Indian motifs and combined them with local ones,

Yijing was impressed by the flourishing condition of Buddhism in Srivijaya at this time, by its large community of monks and the high standard of Buddhist scholarship practiced there—so much so that he urged other Buddhist pilgrims to spend time in Srivijaya in order to improve their Sanskrit there before proceeding to India. He also noticed that Sumatran Buddhism possessed some unique characteristics. The *Jatakamala* or "Garland of Birth Stories" was chanted out loud, and prayers were offered to *nagas* ("serpent deities") and other spirits during fasting ceremonies.

Yijing gives accounts of many other Chinese pilgrims who went to study in Indonesia. Besides Sanskrit, they also learned the vernacular language. Some found life so congenial there that they remained behind permanently. At least one of Yijing's contemporaries forsook monastic life completely and married an Indonesian, thus becoming the first known Chinese to emigrate to Indonesia.

Indonesia also attracted Buddhist scholars from India. Yijing reports that monks from Sichuan and Tonkin went to Java in order to study under a famous Indian teacher. One of the most important Buddhist thinkers of the eighth century, Vajrabodhi, was born in Kanci, South India, around A.D. 670. He studied and perhaps revised two texts, the *Mahavairocana* or "Great Vairocana Scripture" and the *Vajrasekhara* or "Diamond Crown Scripture," both of which became very important in Java. Young Vajrabodhi received supernatural instructions to spread these texts to China. He sailed to Sumatra in 717 then continued on to Java. He was still in Java in 718 when he met a 14-year-old Sri Lankan monk named Amoghavajra who had come to Java on a trading visit with his uncle. Amoghavajra became Vajrabodhi's pupil and accompanied him to China in 719.

They stayed in China until Vajrabodhi's death in 741. Amoghavajra then made another trip to Java, where he collected new scriptures to take back to China and translate into Chinese. Amoghavajra attracted disciples in China, one of whom, Huiguo (746-805), continued his teachings. Among Huiguo's pupils were a Javanese known to us as Bianhung, and a Japanese, Kobo Daishi, who later founded the Shingon or "True Word" sect of Buddhism in Japan. Scholars believe that Shingon and ancient Javanese Buddhism are closely related. Certainly Indonesian and Shingon statues share many similarities.[6]

Partly as a result of cultural contacts fostered by pilgrims such as these, Buddhism enjoyed a short but intense period of popularity in central Java. All known Buddhist temples there, including Borobudur, were built

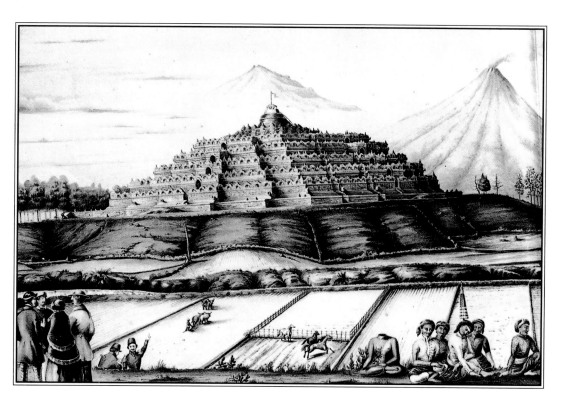

A drawing of Borobudur by F.C. Wilsen dating from ca. 1850. Interesting details include the teahouse and flag atop the central stupa, and the portraits of European and Javanese visitors to the monument in the foreground.

within a century of one another, between A.D. 750 and 850. Buddhism remained the principal religion in Sumatra for a much longer period. In 1013 a 31-year-old Indian named Atisa who had been ordained in India traveled to Srivijaya in order to study with a famous teacher. Atisa stayed in Srivijaya for 20 years, and then in 1038 at the age of 56, he was invited to Tibet where he became known as Dipankara Srijnana, and is credited with reshaping Tibetan Buddhism before his death in 1054.

A text found in Tibet known as the *Sarva Durgati Parisodhana* or "Elimination of all Evil Rebirths" is quite distinct from usual Tibetan works. At least one expert suspects it came from Srivijaya.[7] Even today Tibetan Buddhism seems to reflect some ancient Indonesian beliefs and practices.

Buddhism in Java

Buddhism was not in a calm, stable state during the eighth and ninth centuries when Borobudur was built. On the contrary, this was a period of intense intellectual activity. Buddhists had high hopes for their religion, and held in high esteem those philosophers who advanced new religious theories and methods. Each teacher and each country where new forms of Buddhism were developed evolved some special interpretations of the religion.

A romantic view of Borobudur by H.N. Sieburgh, one of the more accomplished painters to visit the monument in the mid-1800s. The artist depicted himself in the left foreground.

Indonesians must have contributed their own concepts in addition to helping spread those from India, but unfortunately very few manuscripts have survived to show us what these were.

Many of the clues must therefore come from a study of Buddhist texts and practices outside of Indonesia at this time. Many Esoteric Buddhists were then making use of practices which were being codified in *tantras* or spiritual "manuals." Tantric practices were well established in Indonesia even before Borobudur was built. Ceremonies involving drinking, feasting, dancing on cremation grounds and ritual love-making were frequently conducted here, especially during the fourteenth century in eastern Java and Sumatra.

Some scholars have argued that Borobudur was not influenced by Tantric beliefs because the relief panels do not depict erotic ceremonies or demonic gods, but in fact *tantras* were of many types, and the earlier forms were often more gentle. Several aspects of Borobudur, such as the placement of the six types of Buddha statues, clearly demonstrate that its builders followed a number of Tantric precepts whether or not these already belonged to a standardized system.

Characteristics of Tantric Buddhism *Tantras* contain practical instructions on how to accomplish a specific task. They evolved in India from popular beliefs in magic and spells that are even older than Buddhism. They are of many kinds, but all advise devotees how to achieve quick spiritual liberation and worldly powers by taking medicines, performing rituals, and doing mental and physical exercises. Yogic exercises began to appear in some Mahayana sects by the fourth century A.D. Sumatran inscriptions from the late seventh century already refer to *siddhayatra* or "pilgrimages to sacred spots to perform rituals aimed at obtaining success." By the end of the ninth century the *Vajrayana* or "Way of the Thunderbolt" which promised quick liberation through Tantric practices had become very popular in Java (*see Appendix C, "Thunderbolts"*).

One of the principal characteristics of *tantras* is the attention they pay to the body. The more austere sects of Buddhism treat the body as nothing but an illusion and a hindrance. *Tantras* view the body in a more favorable light, considering it to be a reflection of divinity and arguing that mind and body cannot be separated but are merely different aspects of one all-embracing reality. On a more general level, *tantras* assume that all opposing forces are ultimately connected and that harmony can be achieved by reconciling them. Thus *tantras* argue that the body should be cultivated to help attain liberation.

As Esoteric Buddhism evolved during the seventh to the tenth centuries, manuals became more elaborate and the use of some of them became restricted. Many doctrines which emerged in the *Vajrayana* were supposed to be kept secret from the uninitiated and only divulged to those whom the teachers judged to be suitable.

As more *tantras* were compiled, teachers divided them into four categories. The lower two levels were for people who needed statues of deities since they could not visualize them unaided. A master allocated a specific deity to such people—gentle deities for the weak; violent and even demonic ones for stronger personalities, with the characteristics of the deities corresponding to qualities which the devotee must attempt to conquer. The third and fourth levels were meant for people who no longer needed icons to envision the deities. Borobudur's structure appears to incorporate this idea of categories because the lower levels have very clear illustrations whereas the upper levels are more abstract.

The Kings of Ancient Java

Buddhism was less popular than Hinduism in ancient Java. The earliest statues and temples found on the island are dedicated to Siva and Visnu. The Hindu *Ramayana*

Old Javanese Buddhist Texts

Early Javanese and Sumatran centers of Buddhist learning must have had large libraries, but the records consisted of palm leaves and other perishable materials and nothing remains of them. We can only guess at their contents by studying a few short inscriptions preserved on more durable materials, and several Buddhist manuscripts composed in Java long after the time of Borobudur.

The oldest extant Buddhist text from Indonesia is an inscription engraved on a set of eleven rectangular gold plates. It is not known where they were discovered because when they were first brought to notice after World War II they were already in the Museum Nasional in Jakarta.[8]

The writing style shows that the plates were copied from an earlier version sometime between A.D. 650 and 800. The text is taken from a scripture which reached Java in the early fifth century, perhaps brought by Prince Gunavarman of Kashmir. It is written in Sanskrit, deliberately simplified by the absence of complicated grammatical constructions. This style seems to have been devised for commoners rather than for priests or religious specialists. Eight of the plates are inscribed on both sides with verses from a well-known Buddhist treatise which describe twelve causes of suffering and the links between them. It concludes that if one of the causes can be eliminated, then the chain will be broken and the rest will vanish.

Two of the plates are inscribed with shorter Buddhist credos. The last plate is incised with some mystical signs. The entire set of eleven plates was probably intended to be deposited as a talisman in a monument such as a stupa, rather than to be read.

Inscriptions from the Borobudur Period Historians have discovered only two documents which may have been written about Borobudur while it was still "alive." An inscription dated A.D. 824 mentions a religious edifice built by King Samaratungga. The inscription is broken, but the fragments seem to refer to a structure divided into ten parts. The number 10 symbolizes the stages of development through which a bodhisattva must pass in order to become a Buddha. The ten circumambulations performed by pilgrims to see the reliefs on the galleries of Borobudur suggest that its builders incorporated this symbolism.

The other inscription records an occasion in A.D. 842 when a certain Queen Sri Kahulunan allocated revenue from a village to support a sanctuary named *Bhumisambhara*, "the accumulation of virtue on the (10) stages." One theory proposes that the full name of the sanctuary, not mentioned in the inscription, would have had the suffix -*bhudhara* meaning "mountain." The name Borobudur might then have derived from the last few syllables of the phrase *bhumisambhara [-bhudhara]*.[9]

We cannot be certain, however, that these two inscriptions refer to Borobudur. Scholars have been forced to cast their nets very wide to capture information from other sources that may offer some indication of the ideas which inspired Borobudur's construction.

After Borobudur The next oldest Javanese text on Buddhism is the *Sang Hyang Kamahayanikan* or "Venerable Great Vehicle" It was composed around A.D. 925-950 and consists of 42 verses in Sanskrit with commentary in Javanese. Its authors clearly drew on the *Mahavairocana* text, which was probably found in most monastic libraries in Java and Sumatra during the ninth century. It speaks of a deity known as Vairocana, literally "Universal Light." Vairocana was originally an alternate name for Buddha, though later Esoteric Buddhists believed that Buddha was merely Vairocana's manifestation in a physical form, for the benefit of those who had low powers of understanding and needed concrete images to help them progress toward salvation.

The *Mahavairocana* is aimed at those who believe in the usefulness of spiritual aids such as mandalas and *tantras*. This scripture had become popular in Central Java by A.D. 900. To what extent it influenced Borobudur's builders is very difficult to ascertain. At one time it was believed that the *Sang Hyang Kamahayanikan* was the guide followed by Borobudur's designers, but it now appears that the monument's symbolism deviates from the doctrines expressed in this text in several important respects, and it therefore may not provide direct clues to Borobudur's design. In any case, it was written at least 75 years after the construction of Borobudur was completed.

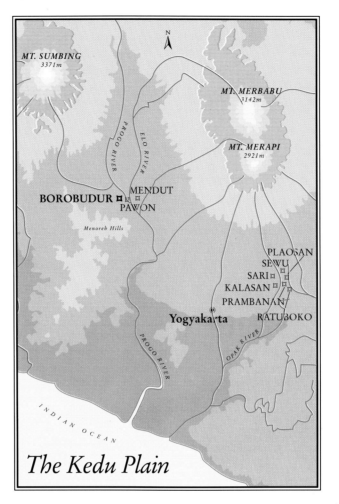

The Kedu Plain

(map labels) MT. SUMBING 3371m · MT. MERBABU 3142m · MT. MERAPI 2921m · PROGO RIVER · ELO RIVER · MENDUT · BOROBUDUR · PAWON · Menoreh Hills · PLAOSAN · SEWU · SARI · KALASAN · PRAMBANAN · Yogyakarta · RATUBOKO · PROGO RIVER · OPAK RIVER · INDIAN OCEAN · N

and *Mahabharata* epics were very popular and remain so in Java to this day. Ancient kings of Java claimed to be able to call upon these gods to bring fertility to the soil and to conquer their enemies. Buddhism did, however, have powerful royal patrons and both religions were linked to two families who formed the ruling elite of Javanese society during the Borobudur period: the Sanjaya and the Sailendra.

The meaning of the word "family" in ancient Java must be explained. The Javanese have never found it necessary to use family names, and Javanese society does not restrict its concepts of inheritance and descent to a single link, such as that between fathers and sons. Instead the Javanese trace their family relationships through both males and females. Groups of kinsmen coalesce around distinguished forebears while less important ancestors are quickly forgotten.

Buddhism in Indonesia was closely linked to an influ-ential family known as the Sailendra or "Lords of the Mountain." This title clearly indicates that the family claimed an intimate relationship with the supernatural power which the Javanese believed hovered around mountain peaks. We cannot now retrace the individual threads which the Sailendra wove into a tapestry of polit-ical relations stretching all the way from central Java to Sumatra and the Malay Peninsula, but they must have included many people more or less distantly related rather than a small clan.

The Sailendra became the dominant political family in Java around A.D. 780, when they displaced another group known as the Sanjaya. The Sanjaya were an older elite who were devotees of Hinduism and had been important since at least A.D. 732—the date of the earliest known inscription to mention a kingdom in central Java, in which a King Sanjaya is mentioned. The inscription was found on Mt. Wukir, which lies just ten kilometers to the southeast of Borobudur.

Tension between members of the Sailendra and Sanjaya families must have stemmed from a competition for political status, but probably had no effect on reli-gious practices. Religion has never been a source of con-tention or conflict among the Javanese. The two families intermarried with the result that the children could give their loyalty to either the Sailendra or the Sanjaya. Their choice expressed political and social allegiance rather than involuntary membership in a clan determined by genea-logical rules.

The Revival of the Sanjaya In A.D. 832 the Sailendra queen, Sri Kahulunan, married a Sanjaya known as Rakai Pikatan. Pikatan gave donations to various Buddhist sanctuaries, including the beautiful Plaosan, but devoted his greatest resources and energy to the construction of the stunning Hindu complex at Prambanan that is known now as Loro Jonggrang.

Pikatan's reign was not entirely peaceful. Inscriptions and legends allude to war with a Sailendran prince, Balaputra, who aspired to become paramount ruler. The prince was defeated and fled to Sumatra. After about A.D. 850 the Sanjaya held supreme power in Java, and without the support of the Sailendra no more great Buddhist monuments were built on the island.

Central Javanese civilization itself did not flourish much longer, in any case. No inscriptions were carved after A.D. 928, nor were any more temples, Buddhist or Hindu, built in Kedu after this time. We do not know why the highly accomplished civilization of central Java came to a sudden and complete end. Later records refer only vaguely to a "calamity." Perhaps a volcano suddenly erupted and destroyed the palace or the Sailendra took revenge by launching a sudden attack from Sumatra. Other possible sources of disaster such as disease and drought have been proposed, but the truth remains unknown. Another civilization gradually arose in eastern Java, but built no monuments on the scale that the central Javanese attained in the ninth century.

Building Borobudur

Since no documents give us specific information about Borobudur, we must approach the problem of its place in central Javanese civilization from a different direction. What political and economic conditions shaped the lives of ordinary Javanese around A.D. 800? What do we know about Javanese nobility such as Samaratungga and Sri Kahulunan?

Borobudur, it turns out, tells us far more about the ancient Javanese than Javanese history can tell us about Borobudur. The monument is built of over a million blocks of stone laboriously hauled up a hill from a nearby riverbed, then cut and carved with great artistry. This in itself is significant, for it demonstrates that Javanese society in A.D. 800 produced enough surplus to support a great deal of activity which did not produce direct economic benefits. The Javanese must have had abundant manpower to haul the stones, skilled craftsmen to carve them, efficient agriculture to provide food for these workers, and well-organized institutions to coordinate such an ambitious and complex project. Above all, it is highly significant that they chose to devote a major portion of their resources to the construction of a monument which, although it perhaps served several purposes, was principally a visual aid for teaching a gentle philosophy of life. Certainly this qualifies ancient Java as one of the most humanistic societies in history.

No traces of ancient palaces or even cities have been found in central Java, leading historians to believe that the Javanese lived in villages of approximately equal size, and that most of the inhabitants made their living as farmers. The fertile soil and plentiful water of the Kedu Plain surrounding Borobudur must have supported a prosperous farming population, and this may have been what attracted the monument's builders to this site. Buddhist sanctuaries usually included monasteries whose monks depended for food on contributions from the surrounding population. Archaeological evidence shows that a flourishing community of laymen as well as clergy lived in Borobudur's environs.

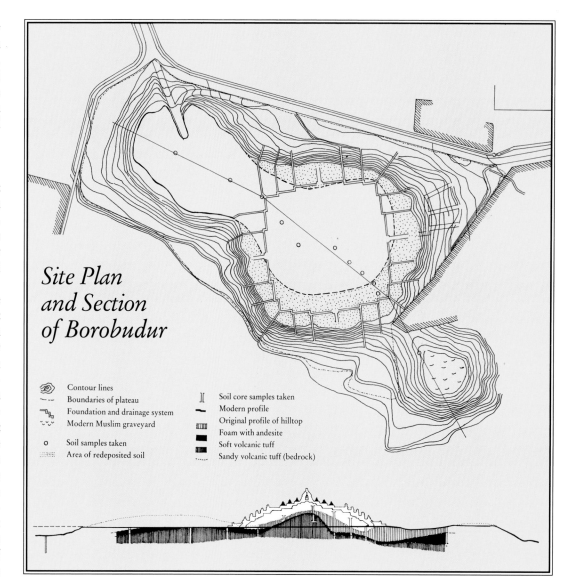

Site Plan and Section of Borobudur

Contour lines
Boundaries of plateau
Foundation and drainage system
Modern Muslim graveyard

○ Soil samples taken
Area of redeposited soil

Soil core samples taken
Modern profile
Original profile of hilltop
Foam with andesite
Soft volcanic tuff
Sandy volcanic tuff (bedrock)

From Riverbed to Hilltop It is impossible to calculate how much it cost the Javanese to build Borobudur in terms of labor and materials. Stone was plentiful and did not have to be transported far. The workmen probably used wooden carts drawn by bullocks to haul boulders from the nearby riverbed up to the worksite, where they carved it with iron chisels and hammers. The principal resources required were labor and food.

Construction at Borobudur probably began around A.D. 760 and seems to have been completed by about 830. Work was probably not always kept up at the same rate during this 70-year period, but proceeded in spurts. At some times many men must have been employed, at oth-

Opposite: *Small but beautiful temples lie scattered over much of Java, including the upper slopes of volcanoes, but the grandest monuments are found in the island's fertile southern-central plains: the Kedu Plain west of Mt. Merapi, and the Prambanan Plain to the east of the volcano.*

Above: *Geological and archaeological studies of the ground beneath Borobudur have shown that its foundation consists of a natural hill which was reshaped by ancient Javanese builders.*

A nineteenth century British engraving of Borobudur, one of many based on Cornelius' 1814 sketches, with elaboration supplied by the artist.

ers only a few, and activity seems to have ceased completely in certain periods.

At least one part of the monument collapsed during its construction. Perhaps other lesser setbacks also occurred, of which we know nothing. The original plan was simpler and required less labor, but the plans for Borobudur changed several times and each new design necessitated more work.

Unskilled laborers performed most of the labor during the early stages: hauling the stones, levelling the earth for the foundation, and terracing the hillside. The monument's stones each weigh about 100 kilograms. If one man with one cart could transport just one stone per day, it would have taken 100 men working every day about 30 years to haul one million of them up to the site. Perhaps another 100 men would have been needed to load and unload the carts and hew the boulders into rectangular shapes. If, as seems likely, they worked during only half of the year, 200 men would have been required to accomplish each of these tasks.

The number of laborers needed to carve the statues and reliefs is more difficult to estimate. A modern craftsman can complete a large Buddha statue in about a month. Thus a group of ten carvers, working at the same pace, could have completed all the Buddha statues on

Borobudur in about five years. Work on the reliefs was probably divided among several groups of sculptors. The masters first sketched the main outlines of the scenes, and their apprentices then did most of the rough work. The masters returned in the final stages to apply the finishing touches to the panels.

Unfortunately, the very last stage of construction is no longer visible except in minute traces. The stones we view today when we visit Borobudur were not meant to be seen at all, for the entire monument was originally coated with white plaster and then painted. The plasterwork would have required skill, for very fine details were molded using this medium. Borobudur would then have appeared not as a dark gray mass, but as a beacon of color hovering above the uniform green of the rice fields and coconut groves.[11]

These rough estimates suggest that Borobudur could have been built in about 30 years by a work force of several hundred men working every day. In reality the rhythm of work undoubtedly fluctuated seasonally to accommodate the agricultural cycle, and took 60 or more years to complete. The construction of Borobudur was a sizeable task, and the achievement of the ancient Javanese is even more impressive when we consider that other temples were being built at the same time.

Some historians have suggested that temple building may have overtaxed the population and led to the fall of central Javanese civilization, but this does not seem likely. The majority of workers were farmers as well as part-time artisans who may even have donated their labor to earn religious merit. Evidence from other temples suggests that at Borobudur, too, they worked in teams, each village contributing a group of men who formed a fixed unit within the overall labor force. Borobudur is not impressive merely on account of its sheer size, but because it shows how large a proportion of the Javanese population had creative talents. The situation is comparable to that found in Bali today, where almost every farmer is also a part-time artisan.

Who controlled the project? Religious authorities and architects probably supervised the daily activities, but the stimulus and material support for the project must have come from the ruler himself. Even if Borobudur were built with the purest of religious motives, such a huge project could not avoid political connotations.

In India and China the construction of stupas was sometimes motivated by political considerations. The emperor Asoka is said to have built 84,000 stupas throughout India as an act of merit, but perhaps they also

For the Elite or for the Masses?

One of the many controversies surrounding Borobudur concerns whether the monument was open to anyone, or whether only certain people were admitted to its galleries. Some scholars have suggested that Borobudur was meant to inculcate the masses with Buddhist teachings; others have argued that only the most illustrious people in the kingdom were allowed to stand upon the round upper terraces, where the spirits of gods and ancestors were thought to descend on solemn occasions.

The *Lotus Sutra*, one of the earliest Buddhist texts to be propagated outside India, teaches that not all beings are eligible to receive the highest wisdom. However, the idea that Buddhists should be divided into several groups, each with their own forms of worship and ritual, did not appear until much later, when Tantric practices attained greater influence.

Borobudur was built precisely at the time when divisions among followers of Buddha were becoming increasingly rigid and elaborate. During the half-century or more when Borobudur was under construction, rituals practiced by the Javanese elite became increasingly distinct from those current among the masses. Our problem is to discover whether such distinctions existed when Borobudur was built, and whether the shape of the monument resulted from the need for secrecy and to exclude the uninitiated.

Tantric Texts and Architects Several parts of Borobudur, such as the balustrade walls and gateways, could have symbolized levels in a religious hierarchy, and would have been useful for controlling access to the monument's upper levels. Perhaps pilgrims had to be initiated into a higher level before climbing from one gallery to the next. The texts illustrated on Borobudur's covered foot and first gallery (the *Mahakarmavibhangga*, the *jatakas*, *avadanas*, and *Lalitavistara*) were not incorporated into Tantrism, but the most important text on Borobudur, the *Gandavyuha*, is part of the *Avatamsaka Sutra*, a fundamental text of third level *tantras*.

In third level *tantras* the Supreme Buddha, called Vairocana, is accompanied by four *jina* buddhas. Mandalas used by adherents of third level *tantras* have buddhas arranged in a manner identical to that of Borobudur's statues. Many scholars have assumed that the buddha statues in the Mendut temple near Borobudur represent a trinity from the *Vajradhatu* mandala, yet another device belonging to third level *tantras*. This mandala is known to have been predominant in elite Javanese Buddhist circles in the tenth century. All this evidence may suggest that Borobudur was built for devotees of third level *tantras*. If this is true, then people who had not reached this level would probably not have been admitted to the monument.

Other data however cast doubt on this idea. Borobudur's buddha images include a sixth form (the statues in *vitarka mudra* on the fifth balustrade) not found in third level *tantra*. Some scholars have suggested that this is Vajradhara, found in fourth-level *tantras*, but few are willing to accept this conclusion.

Mendut may be mentioned (under the name Venuvana) in an inscription called the Karangtengah stone which uses terminology belonging to the second rather than the third level of Tantrism. Ancient Javanese bronze statues represent deities from several different levels of Tantric practice. The *Sang Hyang Kamahayanikan* combines ideas from two sources, one a second level *tantra*, the other a third level text. The Old Balinese *Sang Hyang Nagabaya Sutra* also mixes elements from third and fourth level *tantras*.

Other systems probably existed. Some ancient Javanese bronze images have been identified as Samantabhadra. In Tibet, Samantabhadra was sometimes considered the Supreme Buddha. On Borobudur the last section of reliefs illustrates the "Great Vow of Samantabhadra" which shows that he was highly respected.

It is likely therefore that firm religious distinctions between people of different status had not yet appeared or were not strictly observed when Borobudur was built. The stairways leading directly to Borobudur's summit, the absence of barriers such as doorways, and Borobudur's open-air architecture all seem to encourage people to attempt the ascent. Some initiation ceremonies may have been conducted on Borobudur, which may have symbolized the attainment by some people of greater spiritual powers, but there is no reason to think that any part of the monument was closed to the general public, or that highly secret rituals were enacted by the elite on the upper terraces.

A bronze statue of the bodhisattva Avalokitesvara Padmapani discovered in the Kedu Plain. The illustration is from Raffles' The History of Java *(1830).*

served as symbols of his territorial sovereignty. The spire at the top of the stupa is often perceived as a nail which physically enables the ruler to keep his land stable and peaceful. In Java two modern royal houses still perpetuate this image of the "nail of the world" in their names—the Paku Alam of Yogyakarta and the Paku Buana of Surakarta. *Paku* literally means nail. A legend identifies another hill a few kilometers from Borobudur as the "Nail of the World" though no archaeological remains have ever been found there. It is quite likely that, in addition to its many other functions, Borobudur also served as a symbol of the ruler's political might.

Asleep for a Thousand Years

Although central Javanese court civilization vanished after A.D. 928, Borobudur was not completely forgotten. Chinese ceramics and coins dating from the eleventh to the fifteenth centuries have been found there, and a fourteenth-century Javanese poem suggests that pilgrims continued to visit the monument, even though it was not well maintained. Was Borobudur evacuated overnight, or did it decline gradually over a period of many years, with fewer and fewer visitors for the monks to guide through the galleries?

The Javanese did not forget Borobudur, but its original meaning ceased to be relevant for them. Instead of a Buddhist monument, it became a strategic hill where rebels could fortify themselves, or a curiosity for a dissolute prince to visit. There is no evidence that anyone still thought of it as a supernaturally powerful place. The account of Ki Mas Dana's capture in 1709 or 1710 mentions only a "mountain" not a monument, but the desire of the prince of Yogyakarta to see the "warrior in a cage" in 1758 proves that some buddha statues were still visible. Earlier superstitions surrounding Borobudur may linger in the belief that one of the statues in the perforated stupas on the uppermost levels brings luck to anyone who can reach far enough to touch it.

By the 1850s, just four decades after Borobudur was reclaimed from the jungle, the Javanese were once again performing rituals here. They burned incense and carried offerings of flowers to the buddhas on the upper terraces and to the "unfinished buddha" which then lay inside the shattered central stupa. They also daubed the statues with rice powder which young women traditionally put on their faces to make them more attractive.

These visitors came to request specific boons: to obtain protection from sickness, to ask for blessings after a marriage and on other important domestic occasions.

The most popular statue was that just to the right of the stairway on the east side of the first terrace, which they called Kakek ("Grandfather") Bima, the second of the Pandava brothers in the Hindu *Ramayana* epic. Childless women in particular stretched out their fingers toward him in an attempt to touch him as he sat motionless in his "cage," or sometimes spent the night in a gallery or on the terrace near him, believing that by doing so they had gratified Kakek Bima.

On the first day after the end of the Muslim fasting month of Ramadan, large crowds of people, Javanese as well as Chinese, formerly assembled at Borobudur. "The galleries and terraces become completely full and the buddha, who is at other times so lonely, visited by very few viewers or worshippers, is completely engulfed by crowds who wander around either merrily bantering or even shivering in fear. They stare at the bas-reliefs, where they rediscover so many familiar objects and faces; they bring offerings and let off fireworks in front of the latticed beehives, as if the time had come again when Buddha fulfilled desires, when he sat on high enthroned in majesty and glory!"[14]

Almost Lost The first reports on Borobudur show that it was overgrown with trees and that the galleries were partially filled with dirt, but the monument was not completely buried under volcanic ash as folklore says. The excavation begun by Cornelius in 1814 continued only intermittently, and the last reliefs were uncovered only in the early 1870s.

Ironically, the soil which had covered much of Borobudur, concealing its beauty, also helped to safeguard it from damage. When the stones were again exposed to the sun and rain they quickly became covered in moss, algae and lichen. The roots of these plants penetrated the surfac, gradually wearing away the features of the sculptures, and the acids created when they decayed dissolved some of the stone. Even though the plants have now been removed, holes and patches of discoloration mark the places where their roots penetrated. White blotches have also resulted from water seeping outward from the hill underneath and evaporating in the sun, leaving behind deposits of carbonates and silica.

Borobudur is not a solid stone mass, but a mantle of stone blocks two to four meters thick laid over a hill, on top of a foundation made level by adding dirt carried up from the plain below. The earth beneath the stone facade was not tightly packed, so water trickling down through it carried away small particles. The blanket of soil that had filled the galleries for many centuries had helped to

prop up the walls. When the galleries were cleared, they began to lean and sag on their weakened foundation.

The monument began to deteriorate rapidly almost as soon as it was uncovered, but the colonial authorities were slow to react. In 1844 they allowed a bamboo teahouse to be built atop the ruins. The first proposal for a major project to halt Borobudur's deterioration was made in 1882 and envisioned taking the monument completely apart and putting the reliefs in a special museum. Fortunately this idea was not taken seriously.

The colonial government instituted an inquiry into the monument's condition in 1883, but found no reason to take action. In 1896 King Chulalongkorn of Siam visited Java and requested and was allowed to take home eight cartloads of sculpture from Borobudur. These included about 30 pieces taken from a number of relief panels, five buddha images, two lions, one gargoyle, several *kala* motifs from the stairs and gateways, and a large guardian statue (*dvarapala*) found on Bukit Dagi—a hill several hundred meters northwest of Borobudur. Several of these artifacts, notably the lions and the *dvarapala,* are now on display in the National Museum in Bangkok.

Opposite: *One of the earliest photographs of Borobudur, a daguerrotype by Schaefer dating from the early 1850s. The picture, of the first gallery, shows remnants of the earth which covered and protected the monument during its thousand-year slumber.*

Above: *To visit Borobudur in the nineteenth century was not easy, but enough visitors made the trip that a small teahouse was constructed atop the central stupa in 1844.*

The van Erp Restoration

Official indifference to Borobudur's fate was only overcome in the early 20th century. A committee was appointed in 1900 to consider measures to preserve Borobudur, and tendered its report in 1902. One of its members was an unknown 28-year-old second lieutenant of engineers named Theodore van Erp. When the government finally agreed to preserve the monument, van Erp was put in charge of the project and proved to be an excellent choice.

The committee's plan was modest and only envisaged protecting Borobudur from further damage. A radical proposal to build a huge pyramidal roof of galvanized iron over the whole structure, supported by 400 metal pillars, was fortunately rejected. It was decided instead that stones in danger of collapsing were to be fixed, the first balustrade was to be repaired, and some gates, niches and stupas were to be restored. The main problem, that of water drainage, was to be alleviated by fixing the floors and gargoyles. Loose stones were to be collected in one place for sorting.

Van Erp began work in August 1907, and spent the first seven months excavating the plateau around the foot of the monument. He found gargoyles, Buddha heads, lions, and decorated pieces buried in a layer 1.3 meters deep. Although van Erp's original orders were merely to preserve the extant monument, he found so many missing pieces of stone—both on the site and in nearby villages—that in 1908 he proposed an extensive restoration of all the balustrades, niches, lower stairs, gates and the 72 stupas on the upper terraces. The proposal was accepted and the project was completed three years later.

Van Erp did not dismantle the monument, but tried to solve the problem of the collapsing walls and subsiding floors by covering the gallery pavement with a layer of concrete. He also rebuilt the circular terraces and their stupas, but because much original material could not be found, more than half of the pieces of the upper 72 stupas had to be made of new stone.

Many stupas had been systematically broken into and damaged by looters who dug as deep as two meters. Apparently precious objects were once deposited in or beneath some of them, but we shall never know what they were. Restorers did find some objects the looters had left behind, evidently considering them to be of no value. One was a bronze image, twelve centimeters high, of a standing Buddha of rather poor artistic quality which had even been broken and repaired. The same stupa also contained two Chinese coins, and nine more were discovered in other stupas. The most recent coins date from the 1403-1425 period.[16] The dates in themselves prove nothing, because coins could have been brought here at any time after they were made, but it strongly suggests that the reference to "Budur" in the fourteenth-century east Javanese *Nagarakrtagama* poem indeed means that the site was still known.

Van Erp did not solve the basic problem of water control. Water from the heavy rains still percolated through cracks between the stones down into the ground underneath it, then out through the reliefs or into the foundation below. The reliefs eroded further and the monument was slowly crumbling both from without and within. The walls continued to sag and tilt until the whole structure threatened to collapse. Another committee was formed in 1929 to monitor Borobudur, but first the Great Depression then World War II prevented the colonial government from enacting any measures to deal with the increasingly serious situation.

Indonesia Reclaims Borobudur

It is fitting that the people of Indonesia themselves finally assumed control over Borobudur's destiny and saved the monument from inevitable destruction. Even before the end of the revolution of 1945-49, the Indonesian government took steps to preserve the monument. In 1948 two Indian experts were invited to visit Borobudur and make recommendations for possible conservation. In 1955 Indonesia requested the assistance of UNESCO, who responded by sending a Belgian expert to inspect the site. By 1960 it had become apparent that the monument's condition was so critical that if action were not taken, severe and permanent damage would result. The government began allocating funds for Borobudur in 1964, but work had to be suspended after a year because of a coup attempt. In 1969 the restoration of Borobudur became part of the first Five Year Plan declared by the new Suharto government.

In 1971 a conference on Borobudur was held in central Java at the instigation of Dr. R. Soekmono, head of the Indonesian Archaeological Service. Due to his initiative and dedication, a major restoration project was conceived. The project tapped a wide range of expertise from Indonesia and abroad. Experts in aerial photography and photogrammetry recorded the exact condition of the entire structure. Meteorologists, chemists, petrographers, and microbiologists were consulted on the best means of treating and preserving the stones. Architects, engineers, seismologists, physicists and experts in soil mechanics

were called upon to study the best way to stabilize the structure. Archaeologists and computer experts were involved in various phases of research and coordination of the massive project.

For ten years most of the monument was closed to the public. Borobudur's principal glory—the galleries bearing the reliefs—was completely disassembled so that a complex drainage system could be installed. Lead sheets were inserted between the stones to prevent water from percolating downward. Vertical layers of waterproof tar were applied between the inner and outer faces of the stones; and drainage pipes were hidden inside the monument to carry water quickly and safely from the building. Massive concrete foundations able to withstand strong earthquakes were placed beneath the entire structure.

Altogether, over a million stones occupying some 29,000 cubic meters had to be moved. All the outer stones, numbering around 170,000, were cleaned, treated, and replaced. A permanent laboratory was set up to monitor the monument's condition, and a Center for Borobudur Studies is planned. All told, the project cost $25 million, of which $6.5 million came from foreign contributions, the rest from Indonesia's own budget. Indonesian President Suharto officially announced the completion of the project in February of 1983. Echoing

Opposite (top): Th. van Erp, the young director of the first Borobudur restoration of 1907-1911, standing beside the sagging stupas before work commenced.

Opposite (bottom): The deplorable state of the round upper terraces ca. 1908, before their restoration. Many stupas had been destroyed by looters in search of hidden treasure at some unknown time in the past.

Above: The 1974-1983 restoration of Borobudur, mainly funded by the Indonesian government with assistance from UNESCO and various other countries and foundations.

President Suharto and Madame Tien Suharto, escorted by Dr. R. Soekmono (on Mdme Tien's left), tour Borobudur on the occasion of its official reopening following the recent restoration (February 23rd, 1983).

An account from the Indonesian newspaper *Nasional* dated 2 June 1953, provides some idea of the ceremonies held at Borobudur up until recently:

"Vaisak Day, celebrated by Buddhists at Borobudur and Magelang from May 26-29 is over. This celebration was the largest since Indonesia's independence was proclaimed. It was organized by the Sam Kau Association, an inter-religious group comprising followers of Buddha, Confucius and Lao Tse. Approximately 2000 Buddhists and those affiliated with them celebrated Vaisak, the most blessed and holy day of the year for Buddhists. Those who attended came not from one nation or race, and included many visitors from Central Java who came out of curiosity to see what would happen. This, however, gave the impression of an excursion, detracting from the sanctity of the ritual.

"People began to gather at Borobudur early in the morning. At 11.50 a.m. the drums played on Borobudur's summit, calling worshippers to meditate. Dozens climbed the stairs to the top of the monument while the drums continued to beat, becoming louder and louder. The committee was busy telling people not to climb the stupas, but they were not heeded, for everybody wanted to witness the Buddhist ceremony.

"Twelve noon precisely, when the sun's rays burn their hottest; an excellent time to meditate. The stupas' pinnacles appeared to soar proudly, except for the highest, which was struck by lightning some time ago and is now undergoing repairs. And the stupas' shadows became shelters for those who could not bear the sun's glare.

"Visitors were also invited to take part in the meditation and were invited to sit cross-legged and face the sun. Praising Buddha in their hearts, they meditated for 10 minutes. Some took shelter from the sun on mats under umbrellas, wearing sunglasses, but all were barefoot."

Another article described the ritual offerings:

"Before the ceremony began, Buddha's blue, yellow, red, white and orange pennant was raised, while drums beat and hymns were sung. These five colors mean unity and symbolize Buddha. After the pennant-raising ceremony the Ceylonese ambassador read the Five Principles which are the basis of Buddhism: 'I will not kill, I will not steal, I will not commit adultery, I will not lie, I will not use substances which may affect my thoughts.'

"Then the *Java Mangala Gatha* was sung by three young girls, followed by lectures and meditations on love and peace, and finally the Offering of Flowers and Fruit was made. This offering is among the most important rituals performed on Vaisak. The white astra flowers and

the words of the famous Indonesian poet, Chairil Anwar, Suharto expressed the hope that Borobudur would now live for a thousand years more.

Borobudur Today

Borobudur is now one of the best preserved ancient monuments in the world—and one of the most popular. Over a million people visit the site annually, the great majority of whom are Javanese Muslims. Most Javanese are proud of Borobudur, though they view it as a suitable spot for an outing, not as a religious site. Nevertheless, Buddhism is one of the five religions recognized by the Indonesian government, along with Islam, Balinese Hinduism, Protestantism and Catholicism. Buddhists and Balinese Hindus together make up about three percent of Indonesia's population of 185 million.

There are several Buddhist monasteries in central Java, including a small one beside Mendut, three kilometers from Borobudur. The annual Vaisaka festival was celebrated at Borobudur for many years. When the monument was reopened in 1983, however, it was permanently transferred to Mendut, where it had been held while the restoration work was going on. Today the government does not permit communal ceremonies at Borobudur, though individuals may come to pray and meditate.

golden bananas, *sawo* and oranges are spread near the statue of Buddha."

Though the great majority of Javanese now profess the Muslim religion, their religious practices vary widely. Some are highly orthodox and follow the Quran literally, but others practice a form of Islam which retains many elements in common with the Buddhism of Borobudur's day. Many Javanese continue to meditate in caves and on mountains in quest of spiritual wisdom. The prophet Mohammed himself is said to have meditated in a cave before receiving inspiration from Allah.

The craggy limestone hills called Bukit Menoreh which rise just three kilometers south of Borobudur contain numerous archaeological sites and meditation spots which are still used today. A spring called Sendangsono just a few kilometers beyond the top of a ridge visible from Borobudur is sacred to Javanese Christians, who often go there to pray. Many disputes over religious doctrines have come and gone in the thousand years since Borobudur was built, but fundamental tenets of Buddhism such as tolerance and respect for life are still alive and well in Javanese culture.

The approach to Borobudur from the east through the Archaeological Park, a walk of several hundred meters. Flower gardens may have been planted on this spot a thousand years ago to provide petals for offerings.

Archaeology of the Kedu Plain

Many ancient remains have been discovered in the vicinity of Borobudur. A government rest house stood for many years on a hilltop northwest of the monument. When it was destroyed during the Indonesian revolution, archaeologists were able to study the site, and at depths between 1.5 to 2 meters they discovered hundreds of potsherds and thousands of bronze nails, a very rare type of artifact in Indonesia. The nails were scattered near two brick foundations and 17 stone bases for wooden pillars. Pavilions must have stood in this area—probably traditional Javanese *pendopo* of the type that are still found on the island.

A large bronze bell and smaller bronze objects also came to light, as well as fragments of statues and a number of ninth century gold ornaments. The latter included three large ear ornaments with round cross-sections, two smaller ornaments with asymmetrical openings, and a finger ring with a stylized *Sri* mark on an oval bezel.[17]

In 1970 four Chinese ceramic jars from the Tang period (A.D. 618-906) were accidentally found when the western side of the hill was levelled at the start of the recent restoration. Other important finds at 1.2 meters deep were two grinding stones, a bronze halo, and a 3-pronged bronze *vajra*, emblem of the thunderbolt used in Buddhist rituals.[18]

Further excavations in 1983 at the southern and western foot of Borobudur's hill yielded remains of buildings (some bricks, stones and small river boulders) and kitchen refuse, including Javanese and Chinese pottery, pieces of charcoal, animal teeth and bone fragments.

In 1974 archaeologists dug 285 test pits near the southwestern foot of Borobudur's hill. They recovered 14,000 potsherds—the largest quantity yet excavated from any site of this period in Java. Some pottery was locally made by beating wet clay with wooden paddles, a standard Indonesian method. The sherds came from twelve different kinds of objects, most of which were for everyday use—such as bowls for cooking and storing food, water jars, basins, vases, ewers, dishes, lids, lamps, and a stand for a large vessel. Among all these fragments, only six complete vessels were found. These were probably not meant for everyday use but were buried intact along with *stupikas* and votive tablets. One or two contained a small bronze cup with traces of some nut-like material inside.

About three percent of the sherds were Chinese ceramics, some dating from the Tang Dynasty, while a number of others were from the later Song period (10th-13th century). Like the coins, these sherds suggest that pilgrims continued to visit Borobudur after the court civilization had left central Java. These recent discoveries disproved the old hypothesis that the main complex for pilgrims stood in the northwestern area.

Stupas, Stupikas, and Metal Plates[19] Many significant religious artifacts have also been found at Borobudur, including fragments of stone statues, an inscribed piece of lead-bronze, silver plates with one-line inscriptions, 252 inscribed clay tablets, and 2,307 clay *stupikas*. The last are miniature stupas varying in height between 4 and 13.5 centimeters.

Stupas are found throughout the Buddhist world and often contain relics and precious objects. Some of the greatest stupas were built to hold relics said to have come from the cremated remains of Gautama Buddha himself. Buddhist monasteries sometimes have "forests" of stupas in which monks' ashes are stored. Such forests once surrounded Javanese temples such as Plaosan and Kalasan. The stupas usually consist of a flat circular or rectilinear base, an *anda* or "body" that is sometimes hemispherical and often bell-shaped, a *harmika* or cube on the top where relics are kept, and a spire, often decorated with a multi-tiered parasol.

Some Borobudur *stupikas* were inscribed with short Buddhist formulae in a script which was not in use after A.D. 900. Such *stupikas* have been found in several sites—at Jongke near Mlati, seven kilometers north of Yogyakarta; at Kalibening (Kalasan), east of Yogyakarta; at Muncar near Banyuwangi in East Java; at Pejeng in Bali; and at Srivijaya's old capital near Palembang in South Sumatra. In 1989 the National Research Center for Archaeology discovered a bronze mold in Palembang which was used for mass-producing *stupikas* of the type most common at Borobudur. Other important collections of *stupikas* have been found in south Thailand and northwestern Malaysia.

We do not know how *stupikas* or votive tablets were used in Indonesia, but we know something about their use in other areas. In Thailand, stupikas were sometimes made by mixing clay with ashes obtained from the cremations of pious monks. Tibetan monks made clay amulets (*tsha-tsha*) with stamped shapes of *stupikas,* deities, or tablets with Buddhist formulae on them. Grains of barley or wheat were sometimes mixed into *stupikas* used in prayers either to ask or give thanks for good harvests. Some *stupikas* were replicas of stupas found in Tibet, and were carried great distances by pilgrims who had visited them. Deities such as Vairocana, Amitabha and Aksobhyare often found on Tibetan *stupikas* were also popular in Java.

The *stupikas* found at Borobudur, as well as the stupas shown in the reliefs, come in many different shapes. A little more than half of them have the more complicated shape of an elongated stupa and are surrounded by eight smaller ones. This is interesting because only one full-sized stupa of this type has been found in Indonesia, in distant Sumatra (Candi Bungsu). There are several types of bases—circular, quadrangular, hexagonal, oval. Only five percent have inscriptions. The *stupikas* are made of yellowish-brown clay identical to that found around Borobudur, and are tempered with sand and a small amount of lime. They were probably stamped out in quantity at the southwest side of Borobudur, but since no molds have been found, this hypothesis cannot be proven.

Some 252 votive tablets—symbols of religious devotion—were discovered in a pit along with the *stupikas* and may have played an important part in the activities of the pilgrims. These votive tablets were stamped with various designs: buddhas, female aspects of buddhas (*taras*), or rows of four or five stupas. In Burma such tablets were made by nobility to earn merit for themselves and their subjects.

Two rolled silver plates found near the votive tablets are inscribed with mystical formulae called *dharani* meant to be recited during rituals. They are mnemonic devices and spells which cannot be translated or understood without additional information. Tibetans believe a person can become "lord of the tenth earth," the highest stage in the ascent of one who aspires to become a buddha, by reciting a certain *dharani* over a *stupika.*

A lead-bronze plate discovered in the same area has a long inscription which has yet to be fully translated. It contains the term *mahavajra* or "great thunderbolt" which is important in interpreting religious practices at Borobudur.

Archaeologists working southwest of Borobudur were under extreme pressure to keep to the schedule of the restoration project. The area where the artifacts were discovered was where stones removed from the monument were to be placed. Thus the archaeologists were often just in front of—or sometimes regrettably just behind—the bulldozers, so that no stratigraphic data could be recorded, making it impossible to reconstruct the history of the site in any detail.

Despite these problems, we at least know that the main monastic complex for pilgrims visiting the monument lay at the southwestern foot of the hill. The pavilions northwest of Borobudur on top of the hill may have been meant for rituals or other activities, since they do not seem large enough to have accommodated many people. The artifacts give us much information regarding the monument's date, the lives of the people who lived in the Kedu Plain, and the nature of religious activities conducted at Borobudur at this time.

Archaeologists have also discovered no fewer than 30 other ancient sites within a five kilometers radius of the monument. Many are marked only by a few brick or stone fragments. Statues still complete enough to be identified are mostly Hindu rather than Buddhist. Several large statues from nearby Candi Banon are now in the Museum Nasional in Jakarta, but nothing is left of the temple to which it belonged.

It is impossible to say how many of these sites were occupied before, during or after the period of Borobudur's construction and use. Probably many Javanese continued to worship Hindu gods even in the shadow of this great Buddhist sanctuary. Much more research needs to be done before the picture becomes clear, but it seems that Borobudur was not built by a society divided into cosmopolitan city dwellers and unsophisticated farmers. Instead it was conceived and constructed by people who lived in very much the same way as those who inhabit the Kedu Plain today.

Opposite and above: *Various types of* stupikas *discovered in a pit to the southwest of Borobudur in 1974.*

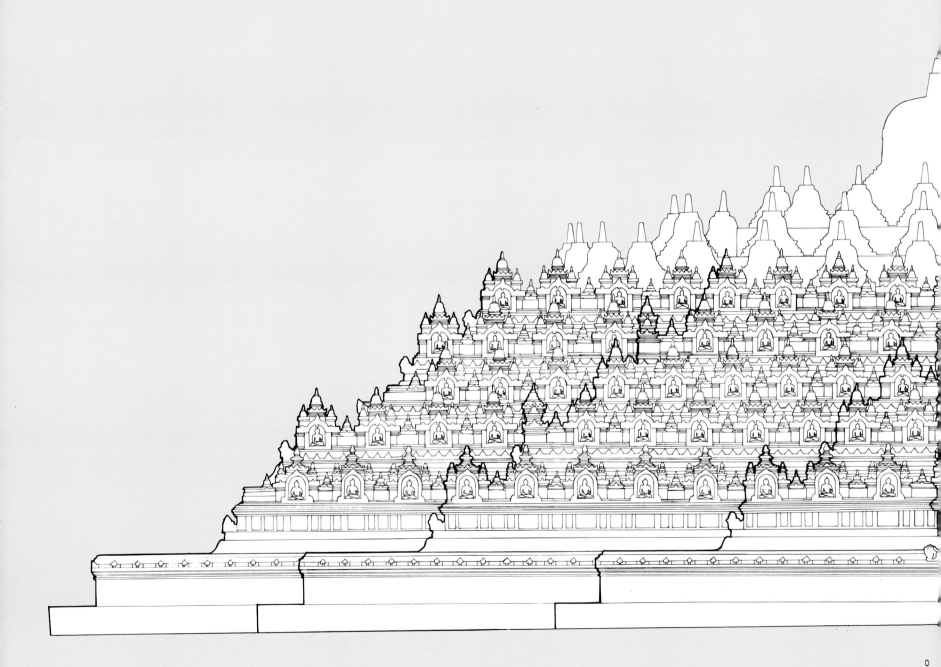

0

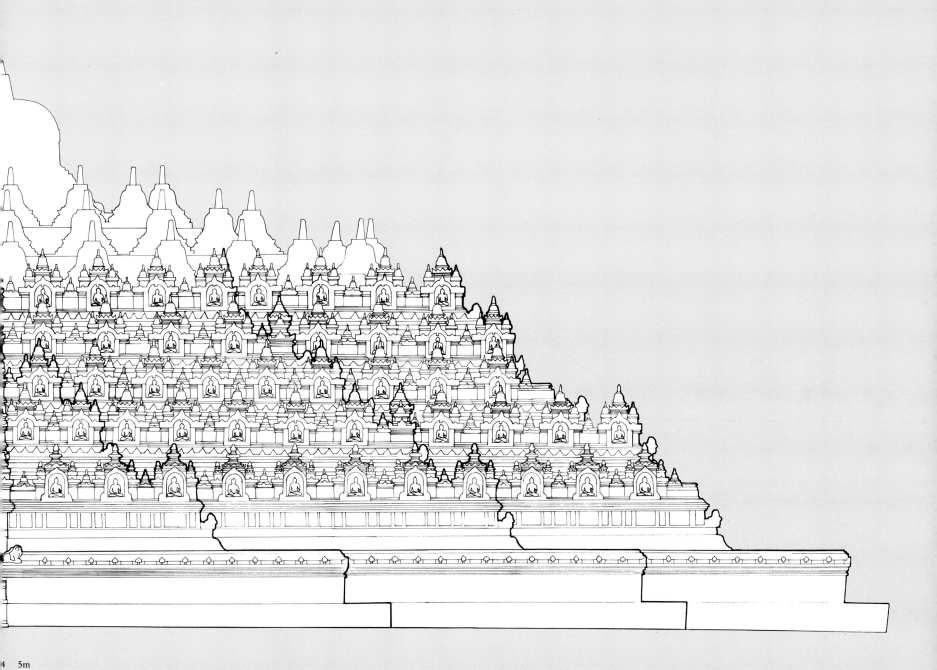

4   5m

PART II

Architecture and Symbolism

BOROBUDUR STANDS ON A SMALL HILL FIFteen meters above the fertile Kedu Plain, surveying a vast sea of verdant rice fields and coconut groves bounded by lofty mountains on all sides. A majestic procession of volcanic cones soars to heights of more than 3,000 meters to the north and east; to the south a jagged array of limestone cliffs marches across the horizon crowned by 1000-meter spurs.

Tropical storms pour two meters of rain on the plain each year. This huge volume of water feeds a productive patchwork quilt of irrigated rice fields and gardens that were laid out centuries ago upon the soft, deep soil produced by millennia of volcanic eruptions. Water not absorbed by plants or evaporated by the hot sun runs into two winding canyons cut by the Elo and Progo Rivers. The two unite a short distance to the southeast of Borobudur then flow 45 kilometers to the south, where they empty into the churning Indian Ocean.

The Kedu Plain is sheltered from the outside world. It contains no valuable minerals or other commodities to attract traders. The only waterway out of the valley leads to a violent, surf-wracked southern coast, which has no harbors and faces no land except faraway Antarctica. Borobudur was not placed here so that it might be easily visited by outsiders. The landscape is thus quintessentially Javanese—exceedingly fertile and by nature focusing inward upon itself.

Borobudur is a monument like no other. It consists of a series of concentric terraces of decreasing size that rise like steps to a central peak. It has no roof, no vault and no chamber; its masonry was laid without mortar. This basic simplicity of form is counterbalanced by extraordinarily rich and complex decoration. Most striking of all, perhaps, are the beautiful bas-reliefs, in all some 1460 carved stone panels covering a total area of about 1900 square meters, with another 600 square meters of decorative carving surrounding them. Set around the monument are 504 life-sized buddha statues carved from solid volcanic rock, while a wealth of other architectural details seemingly fill every available nook and cranny.

The Pilgrim's Progress Ancient Javanese came to Borobudur as pilgrims—to climb this holy man-made mountain and attain spiritual merit. Borobudur provided a place where Buddhists could physically and spiritually pass through the ten stages of development that would transform them into enlightened bodhisattvas. This transformation was the monument's main purpose, and both the overall design as well as the stories portrayed on Borobudur's reliefs are all connected with this theme.

Pilgrims standing before the monument for the first time would undoubtedly have felt awed and somewhat daunted by its looming mass, just as we do today. Borobudur has a purposeful air, as though it is prepared to do something to us should we venture into its maze of stairways, galleries, terraces, and sculptures. Nothing in our past experience prepares us for what is to come when we tour the monument and surrender to its power.

The first and lowest part that we see today is an undecorated square base measuring 113 meters on each side, but this was not how the monument was originally meant to be seen. The designers wanted visitors to see a row of 160 relief panels set all around the base just above the ground, each one measuring 200 x 67 centimeters and

Overleaf: *A full frontal view of Borobudur showing 108 of the 432 buddha statues placed in niches atop the balustrades, which suggest hermits meditating in caves on a mountain top. Visible above them are the stupas on the three upper terraces, each of which encloses an "invisible" buddha that may only be seen when peering directly into regular openings in their perforated stone sheaths.*

Opposite: *An engraving of Borobudur's first gallery, main wall, published in the second edition of Raffles' The History of Java (1830). The depiction of the reliefs, based on drawings made by Cornelius in 1814, does not correspond to any of the actual carvings.*

Above: *An aerial view of Borobudur seen from the north. Visitors on the upper terrace cluster around a stupa containing the statue known as* Kakek Bima, *which is credited by the Javanese with having special powers.*

Opposite: *Top view of Borobudur. The mandala-like pattern of the monument is clearly evident when seen from this perspective. Borobudur has also frequently been compared to a lotus, and the three concentric rings of stupas are indeed reminiscent of the seed pods at the heart of the flower.*

illustrating a scene from a Buddhist scripture on heaven and hell known as the *Mahakarmavibhangga*. The base was decorated with a graceful curved molding and several square projections. All of these embellishments, including the carved panels themselves, had to be sacrificed when the original base of the monument proved too narrow to support it and collapsed. The entire base was then encased within a new and much broader but unadorned mantle of stones. The original base and its decorations (the so-called "hidden foot") were only discovered in 1885, and a portion of it has been left exposed at the southeastern corner of the monument. Here the moldings and four of the relief panels may be seen.

In the middle of each of the four sides of the monument a long, straight stairway leads from the ground all the way to the uppermost terrace of the structure, a climb of some 26 meters. The steps to the first level are divided into three short flights. At ground level to the right and left of the steps are statues of mythical beasts called *makara*s with lions in their mouths. At the end of the first flight these become more fanciful monster heads. The sides of the second flight of steps begin in volutes with triangular designs, a common motif in Javanese art.

At the top of these steps lies an elevated, four-meter-wide walkway that runs all the way around the base of

the monument. Ancient pilgrims performed their ceremonial circumambulations here, and a series of carvings set all along the outer wall of the gallery above (which archaeologists call the balustrade) were placed there so as to be clearly seen from the walkway. These depict celestial beings and guardian demons, as well as jewel trees, vases, conch shells, and other motifs—all symbolizing that the area within the lowest balustrade wall is protected and holy.

Atop the balustrade, each set into its own niche, are Buddha statues measuring 106 centimeters in height that gaze impassively outward from each of the monument's four sides. There were originally 104 such statues on the first level, followed by 104 more on the second level, 88 on the third, 72 on the fourth, and 54 on the top. Many are now missing.

The Galleries A third flight of steps leads from the walkway up to the first level, with its gallery of magnificently-carved stone walls on either side. Although visitors can enter the gallery from any of the four main stairways, one on each side of the monument, ancient pilgrims coming to study the reliefs would first have used the eastern stairs, for it is here that the stories told in the relief panels begin.

Each of Borobudur's four lower levels contains such a panelled gallery. The four trace concentric square paths around the monument, each smaller than the one below it, so that when seen from above they form four concentric boxes.[1] The first gallery is 88 meters long on each side, so that to walk all the way around the first level involves a journey of about 360 meters. The second gallery measures over 320 meters all around; the third is 288 meters and the fourth 256 meters. Thus a complete circuit of all four galleries covers a distance of about 1.2 kilometers or three-quarters of a mile.

The first gallery contains four series of reliefs—two on the outer or balustrade wall (one upper and one lower) and two on the inner or main wall. To see them consecutively the visitor must therefore walk around the first gallery four times before climbing to the next level. The second, third, and fourth galleries each have two series of reliefs, so to see them in sequence the visitor must walk around each level twice. To see all the reliefs in their correct order., pilgrims must consequently walk around the monument ten times, covering a total distance of nearly five kilometers (three miles).

These galleries give the visitor a feeling rather like being in a corridor that is about two meters wide, with high walls on either side and only the sky overhead. The

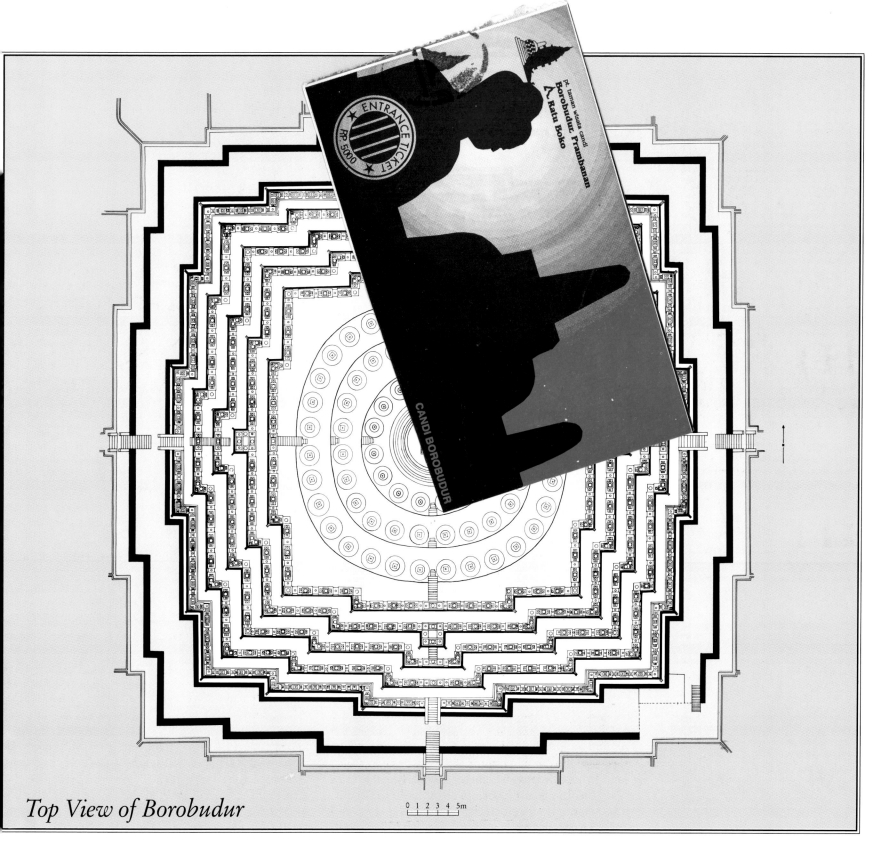

Top View of Borobudur

0 1 2 3 4 5m

The first gallery of Borobudur. Once the pilgrim enters the corridors containing the reliefs, he is completely cut off from the outside world except for a view of the sky above.

and most are beautiful or handsome; those which are ugly or fearsome are also humorous or humble.

The impact of the first gallery is particularly great becaus it contains four series of reliefs—two large ones one above the other on the main wall, and two smaller ones on the balustrade. Every scene is divided from the next by decorative pilasters and ornate scrollwork, each one unique, with bases formed by a wide assortment of objects, people, and animals.

Above the upper edge of the outer balustrade, the rear walls of the niches in which the buddha statues sit are visible. Those on the first balustrade are decorated with a crowning motif representing a jewel, while the niches on the upper galleries are decorated with small stupas.

The reliefs are arranged so that as one ascends the monument, the stories become more complicated and abstract. The upward physical progress of the pilgrim is thus itself a symbolic progress from the "world of illusion" to one of knowledge and enlightenment.

Fables and Fairytales The two series of smaller reliefs on the balustrade (outer wall) of the first gallery depict popular Buddhist stories from collections known as *jatakas* and *avadanas* concerning the previous incarnations of people who later became buddhas. The lower series on the main or inner wall also contains *jataka* and *avadana* tales. All of these are entertaining stories, much like Aesop's fables or fairytales. The reliefs on the balustrade altogether comprise 500 panels of varying sizes. Those on the top row are smaller (either 62 centimeters square or 100 x 62 centimeters) than those on the bottom (260 x 65 centimeters).

The Life of Sakyamuni The upper series of reliefs on the main wall of the first gallery is more abstract. It illustrates the life story of Gautama Buddha according to a text called the *Lalitavistara*. This story introduces the viewer to more elaborate expressions of Buddhist ideas. The panels, which begin on the south (left) side of the eastern stairway, total 120 (each measuring 276 x 80 centimeters).

The Quest for Wisdom At the end of the first gallery pilgrims arrive back at the eastern stairs and then ascend to the second gallery. Here are found two series of reliefs. On the outer wall are depicted more *jatakas* and *avadanas* in 100 panels of two sizes (190 x 55 centimeters and 85 x 55 centimeters). The inner wall of this gallery contains panels that begin to reveal what may be referred to as Borobudur's "main theme"—the example of the pilgrim Sudhana who visited 110 teachers in his endeavor to become a bodhisattva, and who was finally admitted to the palace of Maitreya on the summit of Mt. Sumeru. The

galleries are not straight, but trace four right-angle bends on each side. As pilgrims follow the reliefs, walking clockwise around with the monument always on their right, the journey is thereby enlivened by frequent changes of direction which prevent one from obtaining a view of the corridor extending for any great distance. Most reliefs must be seen up close, from no further than the width of the gallery, although the reliefs at the corners can be seen from farther away.

As one approaches the corner, a panel topped by triangular ornaments called antefixes may be seen. Water spouts placed here are shaped like *makaras* on the lowest level, but at the upper levels, Kala-like faces are used. Above these is a statue of a buddha in a niche, flanked by pilasters crowned by human figures called *ganas* who hold up *makaras* with their hands. A Kala head appears in the center of the arch above the buddha statue.

Entering the first gallery, we plunge headlong into a world of myth. Hundreds of images appear wearing costumes, posturing amid buildings and trees, doing things which seem important but are difficult to interpret. The scenes frequently portray situations rather than actions. Without further explanation it is usually impossible to decipher what is going on. The effect of these crowded scenes is not frightening, however. The faces are serene

Locations of the Borobudur Reliefs

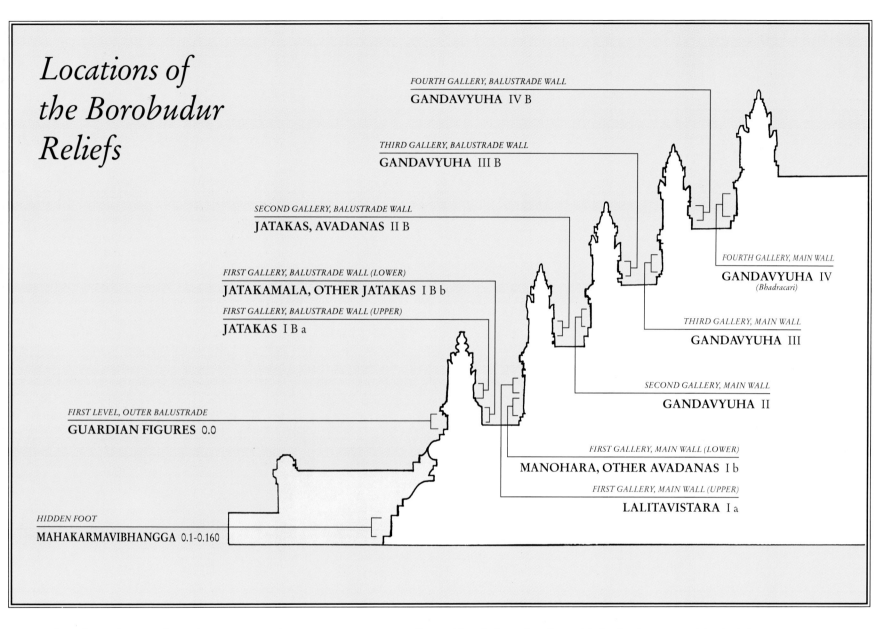

FOURTH GALLERY, BALUSTRADE WALL
GANDAVYUHA IV B

THIRD GALLERY, BALUSTRADE WALL
GANDAVYUHA III B

SECOND GALLERY, BALUSTRADE WALL
JATAKAS, AVADANAS II B

FIRST GALLERY, BALUSTRADE WALL (LOWER)
JATAKAMALA, OTHER JATAKAS I B b

FIRST GALLERY, BALUSTRADE WALL (UPPER)
JATAKAS I B a

FIRST LEVEL, OUTER BALUSTRADE
GUARDIAN FIGURES 0.0

HIDDEN FOOT
MAHAKARMAVIBHANGGA 0.1-0.160

FOURTH GALLERY, MAIN WALL
GANDAVYUHA IV
(Bhadracari)

THIRD GALLERY, MAIN WALL
GANDAVYUHA III

SECOND GALLERY, MAIN WALL
GANDAVYUHA II

FIRST GALLERY, MAIN WALL (LOWER)
MANOHARA, OTHER AVADANAS I b

FIRST GALLERY, MAIN WALL (UPPER)
LALITAVISTARA I a

story, taken from the *Gandavyuha* text, occupies 128 panels on the main wall (each measuring 192 x 114 centimeters except for those beside the gates, which are 150 x 114 centimeters). It is continued on the main wall of the third level (88 panels measuring 130 x 104 centimeters) and on the balustrade (88 panels measuring 130 x 104 centimeters), then on the balustrade of the fourth level (84 panels in two sizes: 204 x 60 centimeters behind the niches, 104 x 60 centimeters elsewhere) before reaching its conclusion on the main wall of the fourth level (72 panels, 250 x 100 centimeters). In terms of extent and content as well as pride of place, therefore, this is clearly the most important sequence of reliefs on the monument.

Entering the Sea of Immortality In Borobudur's original design only the third and fourth galleries had elaborate gateways topped by arches at the entrance, but these were later added to the first and second levels as well. Most of the gateways have disappeared, but some remain—at the eastern entrance to the fourth gallery and the north entrance to the round terraces. The gateways are ornate. A fearsome monster head called a Kala forms the top of an arch through which the visitor must walk.

Reliefs line both the main or inner wall as well as the outer or balustrade wall of each of the four galleries. The first gallery has both an upper and a lower series of panels on either side, so that in all there are ten distinct series of panels. Another series of panels was originally visible along the wall of the base, but this "hidden foot" was covered during the monument's construction.

Above and right: *Gateways leading from one level to the next on the four central staircases. The best preserved of these, on the north side of the uppermost gallery, is elaborately decorated with* kala-makara *motifs symbolizing immortality, and with* rsis *or wise men who shower blossoms upon the faithful as they pass to the round terraces above. Pilgrims reaching the upper terraces after having studied and absorbed the lessons contained in the reliefs may well have been considered bodhisattvas.*

When passing through the gate one seems to walk straight into his mouth, for he has no lower jaw. Instead, flowers dangle from his upper lip, and the gateway is bordered by flames with more *makaras* on either side, facing outward.

The gateways on the different levels varied. Those on the three lower levels were decorated with parrots or *kinnaras*—half-human, half-bird creatures perched just beneath Kala's jaw. The last gateway leading from the square galleries to the upper terraces is quite different, however. The parrots and *kinnaras* are replaced here by *rsis* or wise men shown in the act of showering blossoms onto those who pass through this final gateway into the Sea of Immortality which lies above.

The Round Terraces Ascending from the fourth gallery onto the round upper terraces, the visitor enters a very different realm. The densely-packed decoration, rectilinear shapes and enclosed galleries of the lower levels are replaced by large, simple curvilinear forms and open, elevated terraces which offer distant views in every direction, imparting a liberating feeling of spaciousness.

Placed upon the three circular (but not perfectly round) terraces are 72 stupas—32 on the lowest terrace, 24 on the middle, and 16 on the highest. The stupas are not solid, but consist of a stone lattice constructed in such a way that the entire surface is perforated with regular geometric openings which are diamond-shaped on the first two terraces, but square on the third. Visitors on the terraces who peer into these openings see a life-sized stone statue of Buddha within. From a distance these are invisible and one sees only the outer stupa.

The stupas are between 3.4 and 3.8 meters in diameter and 3.5 to 3.75 meters high. The *anda* or body is bell-shaped. The stupas are topped by spires which stand on bases called *harmika,* sometimes used to contain relics. The harmikas are square on the lower two levels, octagonal on the highest level. These stupas were ransacked by treasure hunters, and may once have contained precious objects beneath the statues. Van Erp reconstructed them but only about half the original stones could be found, so he had replacements carved. The replacement stones are now indicated by square pegs of plastic. Van Erp had marked them with lead pegs, but these were dug out by boys who used them as sinkers on their fishing lines.

At the highest point of the monument, in the very center of the structure, stands a huge stupa, measuring 16 meters in diameter and surrounded by a narrow ledge that was probably intended for offerings. Only fragments of the original central stupa remain—though they give an idea of the simple carved horizontal bands it once pos-

sessed, and the tall spire containing a 13-tiered parasol which once surmounted the entire monument.

Monument With a Message

The reliefs on Borobudur are so beautiful and rich that they can easily overshadow the monument's other attributes. Some would argue that since they received so much care and skill they must have constituted the principal motivation for Borobudur's construction. If this were so, however, the monument would simply consist of a series of galleries in which the carvings were hung like paintings. Further study of the monument shows that there is more to Borobudur than this, and though we will never be sure why the Javanese built Borobudur, the monument's main meaning is more likely to be found in the complex relationship that exists between the reliefs and the architecture, rather than simply in the reliefs themselves. The reliefs form only one component in a larger design, and in order to understand Borobudur we need to solve the riddle of the monument's structure.

Deciphering the Code It would be incorrect to call Borobudur a temple. Ancient Javanese inscriptions refer to religious edifices as *prasada*, of which there were several categories. We do not know precisely how they differed, but ceremonies and symbolism varied significantly among them. Most ancient Javanese temples contained a room where special objects of worship were kept, but the rooms were too small to allow more than a few individuals inside at one time. Perhaps only priests entered the temples. For the laiety of ancient Indonesia the religious structure itself was the icon, which they honored by walking around without entering.

Borobudur is the only surviving monument of its type in Java. Other Buddhist structures have rooms and were designed to house icons. Borobudur's design is so different from these that it seems logical to conclude that its purpose also differed. It was not intended as a place to show devotion to the buddhas, but rather as a place to achieve the practical end of becoming a bodhisattva.

Borobudur expresses a complex message in a code that has yet to be cracked, partly because the range of individual elements making up the code is so vast. Why are there six square terraces and four round ones? Why do the niches on the bottom balustrade have a jewel motif, while those on the upper four balustrades have a stupa motif? Why are the 72 perforated stupas at the top divided into two types: one with diamond-shaped holes and square *harmikas* on the two lower terraces, another with square holes and octagonal *harmikas* on the upper terrace? Obviously all of these design elements mean something, but what can it be?

These variations were not merely decorative. Like the reliefs on the galleries, the upper terraces, statues and stupas all tell a tale, but in a more abstract way so that it is nearly impossible to know which passage in the huge volume of Buddhist metaphysical literature they represent. Undoubtedly Borobudur's master plan also incorporates a number of concepts which are purely Javanese and not Buddhist at all, and so are unrecorded in any of the texts that we have.

Scholars have devoted a great deal of energy to the search for a single concept which would explain every aspect of Borobudur's design. According to one theory, the round upper terraces were meant to form the base for an enormous stone stupa which contained a precious relic of Gautama Buddha. Some have said that a stupa is indeed all that Borobudur is; that its profile, from foot to

spire is meant to suggest an earth mound, bubble, or upturned bowl—all common analogies for the shape of a stupa. If this were true, then the reliefs would simply be decorations for the stupa's base, which is hardly the case.

Another well-known theory proposes that Borobudur has a tripartite structure representing the three Buddhist realms of existence: Desire, Form and Formlessness. But this, too, is probably incorrect.[2] Another speculates that it was designed as a giant mandala or sacred enclosure for use in initiation rites. Yet another asserts that the monument was above all a symbol of the royal might of the Sailendra rulers. Finally, for some, Borobudur represents the abode of the gods, sacred Mt. Sumeru situated at the center of the cosmos.

What is clear is that Borobudur's architectural form had multiple associations for the ancient Javanese—and that it would be impossible to disentangle them completely. Borobudur's design cannot be reduced to a single element; rather it combines three principal motifs: mountain, stupa and mandala. Although each had unique connotations, their symbolism overlapped. Borobudur's designers succeeded brilliantly in linking the three to create an integrated, coherent monument.

The meaning of Borobudur should ideally be expressed in the words of the ancient Javanese themselves.

The plateau on which the round terraces stand. The lions were not originally here, but instead guarded the hillside stairways below the monument.

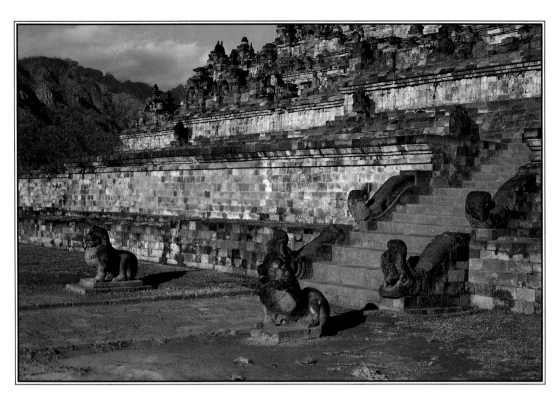

Entrance to the stairway, east side, leading from ground level to a walkway built atop the stone encasement concealing the "hidden foot" of the monument.

Since their manuscripts have not survived, we have been forced to glean what we can from other sources. Like an archaeologist, we must collect as many loose fragments as possible, then try to put these pieces of information together to reconstruct the logic of the monument's overall design. Inevitably we find that some of the pieces are still missing.

Architectural History

According to legend, Borobudur was designed by a divine architect named Gunadharma, whose profile is said to be visible in the shape of the Menoreh Hills just south of Borobudur. Far from having been the work of a single designer, however, research shows that in fact Borobudur was remodeled four times within 50 years.[3]

A group of Hindus or adherents of a pre-Indic faith had already begun to erect a large structure on Borobudur's hill before the site was appropriated by Buddhists. For this monument, workers cut terraces into the sides of the hill and carried soil up to the top to form a broad plateau around a central peak. Then they erected a massive stone structure with three levels which correspond to the first three levels of the later Buddhist monument.

We do not know what this building represented. Archaeologists have discovered large man-made terraces in several parts of Java, some with elaborate stone facings and upright monolithic slabs. A few were built in prehistoric times and might have been used for rituals to obtain supernatural power from the ancestors. Modern equivalents, called *punden,* are still found on hilltops near old villages and are believed to be sites where village founders were buried. *Bersih desa* ("cleaning the village") ceremonies are traditionally held in them to purge evil influences with the ancestors' help.

The first builders left foundations which are unlike any in later Hindu and Buddhist shrines. Borobudur's unusual form is partly due to the need to accommodate this earlier foundation, and it may therefore be considered more Javanese than Buddhist or Hindu.

We shall never know what the original architects intended since they never completed their work, and later remodeling obliterated many of its details. Neither can we determine the precise date when the initial building activity took place, though it was probably around A.D. 760 or 770. There is no evidence that the first builders were forcibly evicted from the hill, and the site may even have lain abandoned for a few years before the Buddhists chose it for their grandest architectural work.

Construction on this hill resumed some time around A.D. 780. Enough remains of the earlier foundation to show that five more stories were added on top of the original structure. Masons added walls and sculptors began carving the relief panels that we see today. Then disaster struck. The foundation proved too weak to support the great weight of the building and some sections of it suddenly collapsed.

The designers could have compromised their original plan simply by reducing the height of the monument, but instead they chose to widen the base. This meant sacrificing the whole series of newly-carved reliefs on the original base. These were covered up and some were even hacked off so new stones could be stacked tightly against the old wall. This suggests that the builders considered the upper portion of the building to be more important than the lower part, even though the reliefs of what is now called the "hidden foot" were carved with great artistry. By widening the base, the workers created a broad elevated walkway all around the foot of the monument. This is consistent with the remodeling of many other temples during this period to include an enclosed walkway where people could perform the ceremony of circumambulating a statue placed in a central chamber.

Most traces of the earliest Buddhist structures in central Java have been lost due to major renovations carried out on all of them around A.D. 800, and as a result it is difficult to obtain a clear picture of early Buddhist architectural styles in Java. Borobudur's architectural history shows that it grew organically over a period of at least 50 years, changing frequently in response to new ideas which appeared in Buddhism during the late eighth and early ninth centuries. At the time Borobudur was being built, Buddhism was in transition and Buddhists believed their faith was developing new and more effective methods to achieve spiritual liberation. People were experimenting with special ritual practices, diagrams and other physical aids to attain enlightenment. Some aspects of Borobudur's form were designed specifically for the practice of these new techniques.

It would be far too simplistic, therefore, to expect to discover one fundamental idea to account for all aspects of Borobudur's complex form. The monument has multiple layers of meaning which accumulated during its active life, and it therefore represents a process of cultural evolution rather than a single moment in Javanese history. One of the chief sources of mystery and wonder surrounding the monument derives from the fact that its builders were able to combine such a great number of disparate elements into a harmonious whole.

Borobudur as a Mountain

At first sight Borobudur appears like a squat, gray mass of stone topped with many spires, an outline much like the ragged range of hills three kilometers to the south. This silhouette was clearly meant to suggest a mountain. Ancient Javanese architects were well-versed in the use of perspective to enhance the height of a building,[4] but technical factors along with later alterations have conspired to accentuate the building's horizontality and to reduce Borobudur's resemblance to a mountain peak.

The sides of the hill upon which Borobudur stands were originally terraced, so that the monument appeared to be a continuation of the natural hill, making Borobudur appear much taller than it does now. The original foot of the monument rose straight up to a height of seven meters. The later addition of the broader, lower foot that we see now eliminated the visual effect of this cliff-like face.

The pinnacle of the stupa was also crowned by a tall pillar which, unfortunately, cannot be reconstructed due to lack of parts and precise information as to its shape. It consisted of an octagonal spire tapering upwards with nine plain bands surmounted by a 13-tiered parasol, reaching a point in the shape of an octagonal jewel. Had

these characteristics been preserved, the monument would give the impression of being taller and slimmer.

Mountains were important religious symbols in pre-Buddhist Java and in the imagery of Mahayana Buddhism. Buddhas often chose to reveal important scriptures on mountain tops. The Javanese tradition of building terraced sanctuaries on high places began in prehistoric times and continues today. The earliest temple complexes in Java—Gunung Wukir, Dieng, Gedung Songo—were all built in elevated locations. The upper stories of many Javanese temples were designed to evoke the holy mountain, and Javanese inscriptions sometimes refer to them as such.

Borobudur was erected by a family of kings known as the Sailendras, "Lords of the Mountain." The Buddhist ruler who started work on Borobudur was named Indra, after the god who lives atop Mt. Sumeru and appears in Borobudur's reliefs.[5] The theory that Borobudur represents a mountain is given further credence by an inscription from the Ratu Boko Plateau south of Prambanan, dated A.D. 792, written in the form of a prayer to the "Sumeru of the perfect buddhas," a clear indication that Javanese Buddhists equated mountains with powerful spiritual forces.[6]

Mountains in Mahayana Buddhism Mahayana

The Menoreh Hills, seen from the west side of Borobudur. Popular belief has it that the profile of the monument's divine architect, Gunadharma, is visible in their outline.

A view of Borobudur from the northwest corner, near the spot where remains of ancient pavilions have been discovered.

Buddhists conceived of the universe in terms of a complex system of three realms with a great mountain at the center called Sumeru. Each realm had a number of subordinate levels that were arranged hierarchically. The first is the Kamadhatu or "Realm of Desire" having various kinds of hells at its base. These are depicted in the reliefs on the "hidden foot" of Borobudur. Above these was the level of hungry ghosts (*preta*), some of whom lived on food left as offerings to the gods, while others were ogres who lived in the forest. Such ghosts are depicted in the *jataka* reliefs.

Next in ascending order are the levels belonging to animals, titans, and humans—the last of which consists of four large continents set in a circular ocean and separated from Mt. Sumeru by seven more circular oceans and mountain ranges. The mountains around the ocean where humans live consist of iron, but the remaining ranges are of gold and the other six oceans are filled with fresh water.

Mt. Sumeru's slopes comprise two heavens and 26 more heavens hover in the sky above it. The first six still belong to the "Realm of Desire." Above them are 18 heavens constituting the "Realm of Form" inhabited by gods who have been liberated from worldly passions but still have bodies. They meditate until they ultimately become pure thought and ascend to the four heavens that

constitute the third and highest realm, the "Realm of Formlessness." Here beings are characterized by neither thought nor its absence, since these opposites are reconciled. This realm would correspond to the Nirvana of Hinayana Buddhism.

Borobudur as Mount Sumeru All the pilgrim can see as he approaches Borobudur are hundreds of statues of men gazing impassively in every direction over the surrounding plain. This is a perfect blend of Javanese and Buddhist concepts. The statues in niches suggest Javanese ascetics meditating in mountain caves as well as the gods who live in caves on sacred Mt. Sumeru. The statues suggest that, like a hermit, the pilgrim will have to practice self-denial and overcome physical discomfort in order to reach the lofty central stupa at the monument's summit. Borobudur's structure required pilgrims to walk ten times around the monument in order to view the reliefs in sequence, all the while gradually moving upward, thus symbolically retracing the steps of bodhisattvas who had attained enlightenment by successfully passing through the ten stages of existence.

Borobudur's designers intentionally created an extraordinary physical effect which visitors experience even today. As one walks through the enclosed galleries containing the reliefs, one gradually forgets about the outside world. But as the pilgrim surmounts the first round terrace, an expansive view over the surrounding countryside is suddenly revealed, producing a unique sensation of exhilaration that was perhaps meant as a reward for pilgrims who had made the tiring circumambulation of all the galleries and had absorbed the spiritual lessons of the reliefs. This exhilaration may even have been intended to symbolize the bliss of ultimate enlightenment which Buddhists believe hovers around mountain peaks.

Borobudur as a Stupa

Borobudur's summit is crowned with a large stupa surrounded by 72 smaller stupas. The stupa form originated in pre-Buddhist India as a burial tumulus of earth surmounted by a wooden pillar symbolizing the link between heaven, earth, and the underworld. Buddha is said to have asked to be buried under one. After his cremation his ashes were buried under eight stupas at different places associated with major events in his life.

Another term which refers to a similar structure is *caitya*. These also existed in pre-Buddhist India but were distinguished from stupas as sites where local spirits, including trees, were worshipped. Sometimes sacred objects were laid beside them and when Buddhists took over these sites they occasionally used them as repositories for ashes. Buddha is said to have preached at some *caitya*. The Indonesian word commonly used today to refer to remains of the pre-Islamic period is *candi*, which like the Thai word *cedi*, may derive from *caitya*.

Thus stupas can either be burial markers or containers of precious relics. The relics could be parts of Buddha's body, his bowl or robe, replicas of his footprints, or even something as commonplace as a piece of material with a scriptural quotation written on it. Stupas could be constructed to commemorate a particular religious event, such as the preaching of the Buddhist doctrine, or simply to gain religious merit.

Stupas in Indonesia Many ancient stupas have been found in Java. Candi Kalasan, constructed in the Prambanan Plain around A.D. 780, was once surrounded by 52 stupas (a significant number according to the precepts of Esoteric Buddhism) which contained ashes, probably from human cremations. In the ninth century, 116 stupas were built around Plaosan. Two stupas were built at Palgading, seven kilometers north of Yogyakarta, at around the same time as Borobudur. All of these may have enshrined precious objects as well as human ashes.

Stupas at Mulungan and Cupuwatu (near Yogyakarta) and Tugurejo (near Semarang) are of solid stone and have

no provision for relics. Other stupas recently discovered in central Java include foundations of at least two very large ones at Dawungsari, and a small one at Ratu Boko on the Siva Plateau just south of Prambanan. Archaeologists are unable to determine whether any of these formerly contained relics.

More stupas were built in east Java after the Borobudur period. Candi Jawi, a memorial temple built for King Krtanagara, who died in 1292, has a stupa-shaped summit. A complex stupa still stands at Sumberawan on the slope of a mountain near Krtanagara's capital. Candi Jabung, erected in 1354, was originally called *Vajra Jina Paramitapura*, literally: "Thunderbolt Conqueror Perfection Temple." Its summit also represents a stupa.

Several ancient brick stupas survive in Sumatra. Yijing mentions seeing many at Srivijaya, but few traces of them remain. Signs of two small sandstone stupas were found on a hill called Seguntang near Palembang in the 1930s, but have since disappeared. The oldest stupas remaining in Sumatra probably date from the eleventh or twelfth century and include the Maligai stupa and Candi Bungsu at Muara Takus (Riau Province), as well as several from Padang Lawas (North Sumatra)—such as Si Joreng Belangah, Si Pamutung, and Bahal I. At least 17 small stone objects from Padang Lawas about one meter high, usual-

A buddha figure with hands in the dharmacakra mudra *pose, representing the "turning of the wheel of the doctrine"—one of 72 identical images gazing outward on the three upper terraces.*

Drawings from the second edition (1830) of Raffles' The History of Java, showing exterior views and cross-sections of one of the 72 stupas containing buddha images on the round terraces (above) and the huge central stupa (right). The latter is inaccurate in several respects. For example the central stupa contains two hollow spaces, not just one.

ly called *stambha,* may represent stupas.

Stupas are shown in 28 panels of Borobudur. Some are surmounted by various numbers of sunshades. It has been proposed that the number of parasols may denote the status of the person whose ashes were buried inside it, or the one who sponsored its construction.

Did Borobudur's main stupa contain such a relic? Some speculate that it did. When Borobudur was first described in detail, the central stupa had a large hole in it revealing two empty chambers inside, one above the other, but no relic was found. According to one rumor, the Dutch Resident of Kedu stole a gold image from the chamber soon after Borobudur was "rediscovered" and substituted a broken and discarded stone statue. The rumor has never been proven, however.

Some have suggested that the incomplete stone buddha discovered in the main stupa of Borobudur was the main statue of the monument, representing the Supreme Buddha in a formless state. This theory has now been rejected. Since Tibetans considered it impermissible to destroy any sacred object, they put them into crevices of stupas. Such a practice may well explain the unfinished buddha in Borobudur's main stupa. A bronze tray, a statue of Avalokitesvara and an iron *keris* (a typical Indonesian weapon) were also found here, but none were of great value. Ancient Chinese coins were found in two of the perforated stupas.[7] It is also possible that the unfinished buddha was simply incorporated into the building as filling material, along with other carved stones from earlier stages of Borobudur's construction.

Borobudur as a Mandala

Mandalas are used in ceremonies to initiate people to higher levels of spiritual power. *Mandala* means "circle," but in Buddhism the word came to mean a diagram with pictures or statues of gods in specific positions. The diagrams are not simply circles but combinations of shapes including squares and triangles. Mandalas can be painted on flat surfaces or drawn on the ground with colored powder, though in their original form they may have been three-dimensional structures.

An tremendous variety of mandalas exists and in Borobudur's time at least 3,500 designs were known. Borobudur's layout resembles a mandala diagram in many ways, but no one has succeeded in identifying it with any particular mandala. The famous teachers who visited Java in the eighth century taught the use of two particular mandalas called the Dharmadhatu ("Matrix World") and Vajradhatu ("Diamond World"), both of which became very popular.

The *Mahavairocana* scripture gives directions for drawing the Matrix World mandalas on the ground with colored powder for use in a ritual initiating pupils of religious masters into higher levels of instruction. The mandala centers on three deities represented by Sakyamuni, the lotus, and the *vajra*. Originally *vajra* meant "thunderbolt" and was the weapon of Indra. Although later *vajra* acquired the meaning of "diamond" as well, it continued to be symbolized by a spear-like object with one, three, or five prongs.

Ancient painted versions of the mandala in China and Japan have several features which represent parts of a building such as Borobudur. The outer border of the diagram is a square resembling a wall pierced by four arched gateways, each guarded by a demonic face at the top, with heads of beasts with elephants' trunks at the bottom. The demon is known as Krttimukha ("Face of Glory") or Kala ("Time"). Kala's gaping mouth devours obstacles to enlightenment. The beasts are called *makaras*. Both motifs represent Amrita, the "Ocean of Elixir of Immortality," which the initiate enters when he walks through the gate. The walls are guarded by a wide assortment of beings which the *Mahavairocana* does not mention. Some are shapes adopted by Vairocana to preach to various kinds of beings; others are Hindu deities who were converted to Buddhism.

The Diamond World mandala consists of nine separate mandalas. The central one is sometimes said to symbolize the jewel tower on Mt. Sumeru where Vairocana first described the Diamond World mandala. Directions for drawing the Diamond World mandala are found in the *Vajrasekhara Sutra* or "Diamond Summit Scripture." Only parts of it survive in the form of a Japanese translation made during the Song Dynasty from an older manuscript brought to China from Sri Lanka in A.D. 742.

Vajrabodhi took a copy of the text with him on his voyage to China, but lost it overboard during a storm. Later he translated the parts he had memorized into Chinese. Vairocana Buddha sits at the center of the diagram accompanied by 4 buddhas and 32 bodhisattvas. The outer edge of the diagram is marked by 1,000 buddhas and 24 boundary guards. The Diamond World mandala emphasizes the number five—symbolized by Buddha, the *vajra*, the jewel, the lotus, and *karma* ("action").

The Borobudur Mandala Borobudur's design is similar in many respects to a mandala. Borobudur's form and hilltop location recall the setting of the jewel tower on the summit of Mt. Sumeru. The statuary in the niches on the balustrades which face the four compass directions

correspond to the four buddhas who surround the Supreme Buddha in the Diamond World mandala. The outside of the lowest balustrade illustrates a panoply of guardian figures similar to that represented in the Matrix World mandala. *Kalas* and *makaras* guard the four gateways to the monument.

The texts which contain directions for composing mandalas belong to the Tantric genre. The sequence of texts on Borobudur's galleries parallels the division of the Tantras into four grades, based on the notion that different lessons are appropriate for people on different levels of spiritual advancement.

Mandala concepts were very important to ancient

A Vajradhatu or "Diamond World" mandala, based on a ninth century Tibetan version. Double circles indicate the locations of 37 main deities inside the square and 1,000 deities outside of it. Four vajra motifs decorate the outer circle at the four cardinal points.

West facade of Borobudur, with buddha images in dhyana mudra *on the lower levels,* vitarka mudra *on top.*

Javanese Buddhists, but no manuals survive to tell us about the precise mandalas used and the way in which such concepts interacted with the other symbolic roles which Borobudur played. The answer to the question "Is Borobudur a mandala?" depends on how one defines the term. To classify Borobudur as a mandala, it is not enough to say that it looks like one; we must also prove that it was used as one.

We will probably never know what ceremonies were conducted on the monument, but so many details of Borobudur's construction are consistent with mandala concepts that we may be sure that Borobudur served many of the same functions as a mandala. It was a space from which evil forces had been excluded, where gods could be invited to descend and take up residence, and probably where initiates could be inducted into higher states of consciousness.

Mandala Temples in Java At other archaeological sites there is much clearer evidence to show that after A.D. 800 many Buddhist sanctuaries in central Java were remodelled to conform to mandala principles, and new temples were built specifically as mandalas.

The most convincing case for such a theory has been made at Candi Sewu in the Prambanan Plain. After a major renovation in about A.D. 800, the complex consist-

ed of a central sanctuary with one main room surrounded by four smaller chambers. This main temple was enclosed within a wall. Outside the wall were 240 more temples arranged in four concentric squares and enclosed by a second wall. Foundations for eight more temples lay between the second and third squares. At several hundred meters' distance were four more temples, one on each main axis. Huge guardian statues knelt at gateways at each of the four main directions. All the statues from the central temple have vanished, but there are niches for one main statue in the central room, with one large and six smaller statues in each of the four smaller chambers (except on the east where there was a doorway into the central room instead of a main wall). The outer rows of temples have niches for several statues each.

This design could have been used to house statues of deities arranged according to the instructions for a mandala. The outer 240 temples may have held images representing the 1,000 Buddhas of the Diamond World diagram, and the central sanctuary could have corresponded to the palace occupied by the Supreme Buddha and his four alternative forms with their bodhisattva attendants. The name of the complex, Sewu, means literally "thousand" and may have referred to the number of statues guarding the central sanctuary rather than the number of temples, as is commonly thought.

Several other buildings in the Prambanan area may have been designed as two-storied mandalas, including the main sanctuaries at Plaosan and Candi Sari near Kalasan. In each case the upper floor was made of wood and has disappeared. Both employed the system of three-fold Buddhas found at Mendut. At the north end of the Plaosan complex are the remains of a group of statues which lined the entire east side and parts of the north and south side of a pavilion. This is similar to a system of 33 deities placed in a rectangular mandala at the site of Tabo, North India, built 200 years after Plaosan.

Candi Mendut has only one story. Its relatively large single chamber contains three huge statues plus niches for four smaller ones on the walls. Only one of the three large statues can be definitely identified—the bodhisattva Avalokitesvara on the northeast. We cannot tell who the other two are meant to be unless we discover which mandala Mendut is meant to represent.

Another type of archaeological remain which echoes instructions for setting up mandalas are ritual deposits found beneath many temples in Java, Sumatra and Bali. These deposits are sometimes found in stone caskets divided into nine chambers, or in urns, like the precious objects used in the Matrix World mandala. They contained various types of objects including gold, semi-precious stones, and remains of organic substances. These were placed around the sanctuary to safeguard it from evil influences in the same way as various materials were to be put under the ground in the mandala described in the *Mahavairocana*.

In Nepal, nine-chambered compartments were built into stupa bases in the nineteenth century. Into eight of them such substances as wood, grain, statues, and human remains were placed, while the ninth was used to secure the base of the stupa's spire.[8]

The Buddha Statues

Many scholars believe that the 432 buddha statues on the five balustrades of the lower levels are linked to the 72 statues on the upper round terraces as part of a single metaphor. The statues on the lower four levels—92 on each side—depict buddhas with *mudras* corresponding to those mentioned in many Buddhist texts. The statues on the east side lay their right hands across their knees, palm down, in the sign of the *bhumisparsa mudra* or "seal of touching the earth." This represents Gautama Buddha's battle against the demon Mara when he called upon the Earth Goddess to testify to his many sacrifices. The statues along the south side are depicted with a *vara mudra*, the right hands held palm up, symbolizing charity. Those on the west display meditation, *dhyana mudra*, with both hands on the lap, palms up, while the statues facing north hold their right hands up, palms facing out, in *abhaya mudra*, eliminating fear. On all four sides of the top row are 64 other statues in a fifth hand position, *vitarka mudra*, the right hands held up, thumb and forefinger touching, signifying preaching.

The three rows of stupas on the circular terraces around the central stupa contain a sixth type of buddha in the *mudra* symbolic of the preaching of the first sermon, called "turning the wheel of the doctrine." This symbolizes that Buddha's sermon set the process of salvation in motion. Mahayana Buddhists believe that Buddha first preached this sermon on the summit of Mt. Sumeru, which gives additional evidence to support the theory that Borobudur represents this sacred mountain.

The depiction of six instead of five types of buddhas has posed a problem for scholars. According to Esoteric Buddhism, the Supreme Buddha, Vairocana ("Endless Light"), is accompanied by other perfected buddhas.[9] Most scriptures list only four perfected buddhas, each identified by the direction they face and their *mudra*. The

buddhas on the lower niches of Borobudur face in the correct directions and have the proper *mudras* of the four perfected buddhas: Aksobhya (east), Ratnasambhava (south), Amitabha (west) and Amoghapasa (north). Vairocana is often illustrated in the *mudra* "turning the wheel of the law," like the buddhas in the perforated stupas on the round terraces.

The problematic buddha is the one displaying *vitarka mudra* on the fifth level of the monument. Some have speculated that this buddha also represents Vairocana, but scholars disagree whether Vairocana was depicted with such a *mudra* at this period. This row of statues does not conform to any known system and constitutes one of the main obstacles to discovering which mandala system, if any, Borobudur represents. If this quite straightforward problem could be resolved, it might provide the answers to other questions about the monument, almost as if Maitreya himself were to snap his fingers, suddenly imparting knowledge.

Sermon on the Mount of Eagles The great French scholar Paul Mus suspected that the answer to the problem of the buddhas on the round terraces might lie in the *Saddharmapundarika* or "Lotus Sutra."[10] This text reached China at a very early period and was first translated into Chinese in A.D. 255. Vajrapani ("Thunderbolt

A buddha image on the upper terrace at dusk. Night was an auspicious time according to Buddhist beliefs, when many beings attained enlightenment. Monks probably meditated on the round terraces by starlight.

VITARKA MUDRA

DHARMACAKRA MUDRA

DHYANI MUDRA

Above and far right: *The six mudra positions displayed by 504 life-size buddha statues placed all around Borobudur.*

Holder") appears, but from the context it is not clear whether he signifies a deity later known by that name or some other god such as Indra. Buddha is still referred to as Sakyamuni. The *Lotus Sutra* thus stems from an early stage in the evolution of Mahayana Buddhism. The scripture mentions *dharani*, or mystical chants, but not the five *jinas* ("conquerors") nor mandalas, developments characteristic of Esoteric Buddhism.

According to the *Lotus Sutra*, Sakyamuni meditated on the Mount of Eagles and then explained to his disciples why he had taught them that there are three different paths to salvation, whereas in reality there is only one. This apparent contradiction was necessary because it accommodated people on different levels of spiritual progress. He also taught them that Nirvana is the same as achieving buddhahood.

At this moment a great seven-jeweled stupa appeared, "welling up out of the earth and resting in mid-air, set about with sundry precious objects. It had five thousand banisters, a thousand myriads of grotto-like rooms, and numberless banners to adorn it. Jeweled rosaries trailed from it, and ten thousand millions of jeweled bells were suspended from its top. The scent of *tamalapatracandana*, a kind of sandalwood, issued from all four of its surfaces and filled the world. Its banners were made of the seven jewels, to wit: gold, silver, *vaidurya* ("beryl"), giant clam shell, coral, pearl, and carnelian, and its height extended to the palaces of the four god kings."[11]

The stupa contained a buddha of long ago who preached the *Lotus Sutra* then entered Nirvana, but reappeared whenever the *Lotus Sutra* was preached. He became visible inside his stupa and Sakyamuni went to sit beside him. Sakyamuni summoned innumerable buddhas and bodhisattvas from many worlds—all in fact only emanations of Sakyamuni himself—who appeared beneath nets hung with jewels. The earth instantly turned into a heaven. Cities, oceans, mountains and forests vanished and were replaced with jeweled nets and incense. Humans had to be moved to another place to make room for all these beings. Each buddha and bodhisattva sat under a jeweled tree.

Since they were still far from Sakyamuni and wished to be closer, Sakyamuni created a great open space in which they could all be near. He informed the assembled multitude that he was soon to enter Nirvana and asked who would preach the *Lotus Sutra* after he was gone. All those before him vowed to preach the scripture. A stupa was to be built wherever it was preached. No precious objects needed to be placed inside it for the body of

Buddha would be present. "This stupa is to be showered with offerings, humbly venerated, held in solemn esteem, and praised with all manner of flowers, scents, necklaces, silk banners and canopies, music skillfully sung and played."[12]

The *Lotus Sutra* contains esoteric elements. Sakyamuni says, "This scripture is the treasure house of the Buddhas' secret essentials. It may not be distributed, then given at random to men. What the buddhas, the World-Honored Ones, have kept has never, since ancient times, been explicitly stated."[13] The name Vairocana is not found in the *Lotus Sutra*.

The scripture reaches a dramatic climax when the bodhisattva Samantabhadra arrives on the mountain peak. He is a figure who also plays a key role in the concluding relief panels of Borobudur. He then promises to protect and assist anyone who will keep the *Lotus Sutra*, to appear before anyone who reads or recites it, and to give them *dharanis*.

jewels. The preaching buddhas on the topmost balustrade would represent Sakyamuni himself. In the final relief of the series depicting Sakyamuni's life on the first gallery (Ia.120), he is shown preaching the first sermon in *vitarka mudra*, "preaching" like the buddhas on the upper balustrade rather than in the conventional *dharmacakra mudra*, "preaching the first sermon" like the buddhas in the pierced stupas.

The *Lotus Sutra* may indeed form the basis for the design of the round terraces. The central stupa would represent both Sakyamuni and also the ancient Buddha who, although he is already in Nirvana, can reappear in bodily form. If this is the case, then Borobudur is also a place where devotees can meet ancestors who are still able to affect events in the world, a concept quite in tune with the role of terraced sanctuaries in prehistoric Indonesian thought.

The upper round terraces have no balustrades, unlike those below and may be a quite literal rendition of the "open space" created by Buddha for the myriads of deities who are emanations of himself. The round terraces may therefore represent the earth temporarily transformed into a paradise where the buddhas have assembled. The statues on the round terraces face outward rather than toward the central stupa, suggesting that they are preaching the scripture to us, just as they vowed to do in the *Lotus Sutra*.

In addition to symbolizing Mt. Sumeru, Borobudur may also represent Grdhrakuta, the "Mount of Eagles" where Sakyamuni preached the scripture. The appearance of Samantabhadra in the final chapter links the upper terraces to the final reliefs just below. This suggestion of continuity between the two main parts of the monument further strengthens the theory that Borobudur illustrates the *Lotus Sutra*.

It is still difficult to explain a number of aspects of the round terraces. The symbolism of the buddha statues in perforated stupas may illustrate the instruction that a stupa which will only become visible to beings already "awakened" be built wherever the scripture is preached. This still does not answer the question as to why there are exactly 72 buddhas on the terraces since this number has no known symbolic value. Why are they in the *mudra* showing the first sermon rather than the general *mudra* denoting preaching? Why are the terraces not perfectly circular but shaped more like squares with rounded corners? Why are the perforations and *harmikas* of different shapes? The *Lotus Sutra* does not seem to contain answers to these problems.

The Invisible Buddha How might the architecture of Borobudur have symbolized the *Lotus Sutra*? Mus never completed his study and gave no reasons to support his theory that the round terraces were designed to depict the *Lotus Sutra*.

Another scholar has proposed a detailed theory based on Mus' idea.[14] According to his interpretation, the round terraces of Borobudur portray the section of the scripture which describes the appearance of the stupa containing the body of the ancient Buddha. The central stupa is no other than the one which came "welling up out of the earth" with the ancient Buddha inside. The 72 statues on the three round terraces would represent the multitudes of buddhas and bodhisattvas who appeared preaching, and the pierced stupas convey the idea that only those who have already become bodhisattvas themselves can see the buddhas. The stupas on the upper terrace represent the earth and those on the lower two terraces correspond to other buddhas who were covered with nets of

Photos at center: *The "invisible" buddhas placed inside 72 bell-shaped stupas on the monument's three upper terraces (the one on the left has been left exposed). These can normally only be seen by peering through openings in the stupas' perforated stone sheaths.*

Above: *A celestial jewel tree producing wish-fulfilling gems of countless colors.*

A Vocabulary of Symbols

Borobudur's carvings display a wide range of motifs with symbolic meanings. Even if we do not understand specific stories in the reliefs, we can still identify the main characters depicted by referring to the symbols found in them. It is not difficult to grasp the basic vocabulary of Borobudur's symbols.

The motifs used on Borobudur are also found on central Javanese Hindu temples. The two religions shared a standard artistic vocabulary, much of which comes from India.

Aksamala "Rosaries" Strings of beads were important ritual objects for both Buddhist monks and lay people. A full string has 108 beads, representing the number of sinful conditions which the worshipper should avoid. Lay peoples' strings may have only 30-40 beads. As in Christianity, they are used to help people count the number of times they have repeated a prayer.

Conch Shells The conch was a powerful symbol for both Buddhists and Hindus. In ancient India it was used as a trumpet and Buddhism derived from this the idea that the conch represented the mighty sound made when the scriptures were preached. Conches are found in many locations on Borobudur, both in panels and as motifs at the bases of the scrolls on the posts between the panels. In Hinduism the conch is a special attribute of Visnu.

Fly Whisks These were also associated with royalty and took the form of pointed tufts of hair, either attached to the tips of parasols, or carried alone, usually by women who stand on either side of the noble person whom they serve. Originally the fly-whisks were made of the tails of the yak; in Java probably some other material was used.

Jewel Trees On his travels Sudhana sees "jewel trees called 'treasury of radiance,' which looked like incomparable jewels and bore riches in buds producing garlands and ornaments of celestial jewels and wish-fulfilling gems, and were adorned by jewels of countless colors."[16] Such trees are portrayed frequently at Borobudur and other temples; they are particularly common at the Hindu site of Prambanan, where they are flanked by half-human, half-bird figures called *kinnara*.

Kala Heads According to Hindu legend, Kala

was created by Siva to kill a titan. According to another legend, the head represents a demon called Rahu. Gods and demons once churned the ocean to make an elixir of immortality. Rahu stole some of it. A god cut off his head, striking him in the mouth with a sword, but because he had already swallowed the liquid, he did not die. Thus Kala's head normally is depicted without a lower jaw. Kala symbolizes the elixir of immortality, which is shown by strings of jewels or other ornaments hanging from the monster's upper jaw.

Kinnara These are mythical celestial beings, normally with the legs and wings of birds and the torsos and heads of humans. They appear as main characters in some *jatakas* but often are introduced merely as decoration. They are associated with music, which they are said to play for the gods on Mt. Sumeru.

Lions The lion was greatly favored by Buddhist artists. Buddha himself was sometimes represented as having the voice of a lion—an animal whose principal quality was bravery. Several free-standing lion statues stood on or near Borobudur, some of which were never completed. A particular form of royal

Makaras This mythical beast with an elephant's trunk, parrot's beak and fish's tail appears very often as an artistic motif in both Hindu and Buddhist temples in India and Java. Like the serpent or *naga*, the *makara* is also a water symbol, but *makaras* rarely appear in literature. *Makaras* can also symbolize the energy excited by desire, including sexual desire. The Hindu god of sexual love, Kamadeva, is symbolized by a pennant with a *makara* on it.

Makaras are found on either side at the bottom of the stairs on almost all Javanese temples, sometimes with lions, parrots, warriors or garlands in their open beak. They are also found at either side of the doorways leading to Borobudur's different levels.

Parasols These were very important symbols of royalty in ancient and recent times, both in India and Southeast Asia. In the early 20th century many types of umbrellas were used in the courts of central Java. The colors and number of tiers of each parasol were strictly regulated according to the rank of the owner. The reliefs on Borobudur depict parasols so frequently that we may suspect a similar custom already existed. Many stupas including Borobudur's main stupa were topped by multi-tiered stone parasols symbolizing Sakyamuni's royal birth.

Rocks On Borobudur a unique convention is used to denote the presence of a rocky landscape. It consists of a number of column shapes with chevron-like motifs side by side. The origin of this motif is unknown, but is almost certainly Javanese.

Rsis "Wise Men" This name originally referred to sons of the Hindu god Brahma who became great poets and philosophers. On Borobudur they are identified by their long hair and pointed beards. They seem to have formed an important segment of society in central Java since they are given an emphasis on the reliefs out of proportion to the number of references to them in the texts. Ascetics and hermits have always held places of high honor in Javanese society, both ancient and contemporary; perhaps these figures portray people with such qualities.

Yaksas "Forest Ogres" These are semi-divine beings who live in forests and are usually hostile to men; in fact they usually devour whomever they can catch. On Borobudur they are discernible in many scenes and can be recognized by their long hair (usually in a semicircular array) beards and large earplugs.

Above: *A pair of* kinnaras—*half-bird, half-human celestial beings who are frequently depicted in the panels and often play a central role in the tales.*

Left: *A* makara *head with a lion in its mouth flanking one of the main stairways leading up to the monument.*

throne shown in numerous panels of Borobudur has one or more lions for supports. Lions are also used in panels to denote wilderness. At least one village in central Java in the year A.D.. 902 was named "Lion City." Lions of course are indigenous to India, but not to Southeast Asia.

Lotuses The lotus is found in almost every Buddhist work of art. It often serves as a throne for buddhas and a base for stupas, and bodhisattvas carry a long-stemmed lotus in one hand. A widely-known Mahayana chant, *Om mani pade hum* literally translates as "Hail to the jewel of the lotus." Gold foil lotuses were sometimes buried beneath temple foundations during the rituals connected with the purification of the buildings as mandalas.

Naga The word literally means "snake" in Sanskrit but in Java it normally referred to serpent deities. Serpents in ancient Java and India were usually connected with water and fertility. They can be either good or evil. On Borobudur they are depicted in human form, but elsewhere they may appear in their natural animal shape. Hindus also make frequent use of *nagas* in their literature and art.

PART III

The Reliefs

NO OTHER MONUMENT IN THE WORLD accomplishes what Borobudur does, either in terms of the sheer scale on which stone panels have been carved to tell stories about Buddhism, or in the more subjective way in which these stories, many of them highly abstract, have been represented with such great artistry. We now know that the 1460 narrative panels on Borobudur were created to illustrate five Buddhist scriptures. Although the reliefs still pose many fascinating problems, scholars have solved the principal mysteries regarding the texts upon which they are based.

Various factors made it difficult to identify the stories told in the reliefs. Artists often depicted the same persons or objects differently in different panels, even in adjacent ones. They also avoided showing conflicts, violence or suffering—precisely the scenes that are easiest to identify. The large size of the panels has produced another source of confusion. In many scenes the main characters occupy only a small part of the panel, thus leaving a considerable amount of space to be filled with people, buildings, plants and animals that have little or nothing to do with the story being illustrated. As we often have no way of knowing which figures and objects are most relevant to the main story, it is difficult to distinguish these from the decorative fantasies of the sculptors.

Another obstacle stemmed simply from the lack of knowledge about Buddhism in nineteenth and early twentieth century Europe. When Borobudur was discovered in 1814 very few scholars could read the Asian languages and scripts in which Buddhist texts are written.

Progress in deciphering the reliefs has progressed greatly since the turn of the century, as manuscripts which lay in secluded monasteries and the recesses of caves in China, Japan and the Himalayas have been discovered and translated into European languages.

Reading the Reliefs The first breakthrough came in 1885 when a Russian, S.F. Oldenburg, discovered that the lower set of reliefs on the balustrade of the first gallery are based on stories of Buddha's incarnations found in a compilation known as the *Jatakamala* or "Garland of Birth Stories." In 1901 the Dutch scholar C.M. Pleyte found that the upper set of reliefs on the main wall of the first gallery depict Buddha's life as told in a text known as the *Lalitavistara* or "Unfolding of the Play." In 1917 the Director of the Netherlands Indies Archaeological Service, N.J. Krom, realized that the reliefs on the second and third galleries are based on the *Gandavyuha*, "The Structure of the World Compared to a Bubble."[1] Fourteen years later a Frenchman, S. Levi, identified the scenes on the hidden foot as the *Mahakarmavibhangga*, the "Great Classification of Actions." In 1938 a subsequent director of the Archaeological Service, F.D.K. Bosch, showed that the reliefs on the main wall of the fourth gallery were designed to illustrate a sequel to the *Gandavyuha* called the *Bhadracari*.

Although the major texts which Borobudur's designers used have been identified, many problems remain. The first panels on the lowest level follow known versions of the *Jatakamala*, but only a few of the subsequent panels in this series have been identified. Was another cycle of these tales current in Java, or were the latter ones simply compiled at random from various texts? Why do

Opposite and above: *An unidentified court scene from the* Avadana *reliefs. A king and queen discuss matters having to do with the group of visitors seated before them, who are probably wise men* (rsi). *(panel I.b94)*

Previous pages: *Female hermits; a scene from the* Lalitavistara. *(panel I.a70)*

A nobleman lets fly an arrow at a group of bearded men seated submissively beneath a tree, in an unidentified scene from the avadana reliefs on the main wall of the first gallery. A group of eight men, perhaps deities, look on from the left. Probably one of the bearded men dies and is commemorated by the stupa seen in the next relief, the last of the series, being honored by offerings. The archer of the previous panel now stands sorrowfully beside the stupa. (panel I.b119)

the reliefs devote such a disproportionate amount of space to the last episodes of the *Gandavyuha*? These and other problems will continue to intrigue scholars and visitors for a long time to come.

The placement of the reliefs on Borobudur forms another subject for inquiry. In general they progress from concrete to abstract in terms of subject matter. The lowest series of reliefs, now concealed, depicts graphic scenes of punishment and reward, while the highest portrays unidentified assemblies of celestial beings. The contrast is quite striking, and the intellectual leap from the subject matter of the lowest gallery to the highest is considerable.

It is likely, therefore, that not every pilgrim who began by studying the *jatakas* on the balustrade of the first gallery would have been capable of understanding the elevated doctrines expressed on the main wall of the fourth gallery. Were the gateways decorated with *kalas* and *makaras* separating these levels entrances for some but barriers to others? Were there examinations which aspirants had to pass before being allowed to ascend to a higher terrace?

This is unlikely. It is more probable that ritual initiation ceremonies conducted on the monument itself or in pavilions which once stood on a plateau to the northwest (or perhaps also in the living quarters at the southwestern foot of the hill) qualified pilgrims to proceed to each new stage. No doubt initiates would have been required to demonstrate a certain fluency in the precepts to which they had been exposed on the lower levels in order to be admitted to the upper ones, but these questions would have been formalities to which devotees responded with memorized answers.

The gateways on the first two galleries were not part of the monument's original plan. The *makaras* which decorate them hide parts of the narrative reliefs. The new gateways may have been added purely as decoration, but more likely those in charge of the monument at this time decided to emphasize the transitions from one level to another. The gateways were not, however, equipped with doors that might block one's entrance to a higher level, and thus they are symbolic rather than physical barriers. The stairways and gates on all four sides of the monument in fact enable visitors to proceed directly to the summit if they so wish, further suggesting that the pilgrims' movements were not restricted.

Ten Steps to Enlightenment In order to follow the complete narrative sequence of the reliefs from beginning to end, the pilgrim had to make ten circuits of the monument—four times around the first gallery and twice around each of the next three galleries. It is probably not a coincidence that the number ten equals the number of stages in the career of a bodhisattva.

The desire to maintain the number ten may also explain why the outer or balustrade wall of the lowest level is decorated with two series of reliefs. The upper series was apparently added at a later stage, perhaps so as to retain the number ten when the *Mahakarmavibhangga* reliefs on the foot of the monument had to be covered up for structural reasons.

The ideal of the bodhisattva that constitutes the central message of these reliefs has been important throughout Javanese history. The earliest Buddhist texts from Java, written just after Borobudur was built, focus on the search for a way to become a bodhisattva. Even today, Javanese mystical beliefs continue to wrestle with the same questions that Borobudur addresses: how to gain supramundane power and achieve spiritual liberation.

The only things that changed after the Borobudur period were the techniques used to gain these ends, and the artistic and architectural implements that were required. Techniques contained in *tantra*, or manuals, were already in use in Borobudur's time, but consisted mainly of what are called "right-handed" *tantra*. These involve keeping the sanctuary on the right side during a *pradaksina* circumambulation and abstaining from acts of anger, killing, etc., which early Buddhism considered evil. In later centuries, however, the "left-handed" *tantras* became more pervasive. After the construction of Borobudur, the use of narrative reliefs on religious monuments became more common, although the circumambulation required to view them was in a counterclockwise rather than a clockwise direction. Later Javanese texts advocated ritual indulgence in the five "forbidden things" for initiates who aspired to acquire powers from the highest grade of *tantras*.

Despite their emphasis on matters of a highly metaphysical nature, the Borobudur reliefs depict many events and scenes from everyday life in a manner which seems intended to communicate with ordinary people rather than religious authorities. In between religious imagery, Borobudur provides hundreds of examples of architec-

One of Sudhana's Good Friends; a scene from the Gandavyuha. A human is shown in royal attire, seated in a pavilion with a chest beneath him, symbolizing wealth. (panel II.88)

ture, boats, farming practices, clothing, jewelry, dancing, etc. Visitors to Borobudur probably came from all classes and might have gone there for a variety of reasons. The upper terraces provide space for meditation, but in the lower galleries people would have moved at a steady pace instead of sitting before particular panels. Large crowds could earn merit simply by walking around the monument without entering it at all.

Teachers, probably monks, would have led devotees along the galleries, explaining the tenets of the faith and illustrating their lectures with the carved panels. The journey to the summit certainly took more than a single day to complete, with much time devoted to rituals. Visitors would have performed ceremonies at various stages along the way up and around the galleries. The entire process was simultaneously a physical ascent to the summit of the mountain and an intellectual ascent to the ultimate source of spiritual power.

The Mahakarmavibhangga
Visions of Worldly Desire

BEFORE THE BROAD FOOT WAS ADDED TO BORO-budur, a series of reliefs was visible from outside the monument. These were located just above the ground and served as moral lessons to pilgrims, depicting men and women performing both good and evil deeds and then being rewarded and punished in hell or heaven for their actions.

These themes are still popular in traditional Asian art. Similar scenes are illustrated in a famous series of paintings on the ceiling of the Kertagosa Hall of Justice of the kingdom of Klungkung in Bali, which dates from the eighteenth or nineteenth century. They are also vividly portrayed in an extraordinary set of artificial grottoes in the Tiger Balm Gardens of the Haw Par Villa in Singapore, constructed in the 1930s.

The Text Mahayana Buddhism possesses several texts which describe at length the effects of specific actions. The text which the designers of Borobudur illustrated in these reliefs was a version of a Sanskrit work known as the *Mahakarmavibhangga* or "Great Classification of Actions." None of the extant versions, however, is exactly the same as that illustrated on Borobudur. In fact the Borobudur depictions vary more from known textual versions than any other reliefs on the monument.

This is not difficult to account for. The texts that have been preserved—Sanskrit, Pali, Tibetan, Chinese and Kuchean from Central Asia—are all in the form of a sermon given by Buddha, which consists largely of a technical discourse on the doctrine of cause and effect. A translation of this text into pictures was certainly not easy to accomplish and some artistic license was probably necessary. Also, since the text is of fundamental importance

to Buddhism and is among its oldest scriptures, it was copied many times and was subject to many local interpretations. The version of the text which the Borobudur artists used was probably rather different from any which survives today.

The Reliefs The *Mahakarmavibhangga* reliefs encompass more than 160 panels, each measuring about two meters wide and 67 centimeters high. They were discovered by accident in 1885, and a complete photographic record was made in 1890-91. Thereafter they were covered up again and have not been seen since, with the exception of four panels at the southeastern corner of the monument which were re-exposed by curious members of the Japanese occupation forces of the early 1940s, which may still be seen there today. The panels follow a standard format—they first depict an action, then show its reward or punishment.

The hidden reliefs depict various hells and heavens from Buddhist mythology. There are eight hot hells. In

The four Mahakarmavibhangga *panels visible today at the southeastern corner of Borobudur cannot be explained with certainty and we can only give possible interpretations.*

Opposite: *A picture of contentment. A royal couple with child, attended by guards, servants, and a moustached adviser.* (panel 0.20)

Left: *Detail from the first of the four exposed panels. The left half of this panel is shown on the following page.* (panel 0.19)

A number of people treating a man who is ill. They massage him and bring ointments and medicine. The left side may depict the reward for such behavior, but the precise nature of the reward is unclear. (panel 0.19)

one relief men are shown fighting and in the next panel they are shown atoning for their sin in the Sanjiva hell, where they tear at each other with bare hands that have iron nails while a bird with a metal beak attacks them. The murder of innocents is repaid in Raurava hell, where the criminals are impaled on the metallic thorns of huge trees. Those who commit matricide are punished in the Avichi hell.

The killing of animals is punished with similar severity. Hunters of birds are condemned to walk through the "Sword Tree Forest" where leaves drop from trees as daggers and stab them. As punishment for cooking fish and turtles, the cooks are thrown into a cauldron in the Pratapana hell. Flayers of sheep are condemned to have their heads sawn through in the Kalasutra hell. Even smoking rats from their hole is a sin, punished by being crushed between huge rocks in the Samghata hell.

There is a system of sub-hells also, where sinners walk on grass-like spears or through burning water, or are trampled by elephants for various misdeeds. There are also punishments in the form of rebirth as birds, four footed animals, or ghouls.

The depictions of the different heavens are not nearly so elaborate. These are nearly identical and each represen

tation has emblems of wishing trees and a pair of *kinnaras*, birds with human heads.

These reliefs were intended to prepare the pilgrim to ascend the monument by acquainting him with the difference between good and evil, and reminding him of the desirability of escaping from the sorrows of existence by achieving Nirvana. But even before the monument was finished these reliefs were buried.

Why did the builders not construct another set of reliefs for the same purpose on the outer walls of the new foot? Perhaps some other expedient was adopted to teach the doctrine of cause and effect before the pilgrims were allowed to enter the upper terraces to view the scenes of enlightenment.

The Inscriptions On the molding above the second exposed panel from the right is a word in Old Javanese script, *virupa*, meaning "the deformed, ugly one." This is one example of about 40 such short inscriptions found above some *Mahakarmavibhangga* panels. These inscriptions were carved when the panels were being designed in the late eighth century.

Their significance is still in dispute. It seems that originally all the panels in this series had short inscriptions above them, but most were chipped off. Some scholars have speculated that these were meant as directions to the sculptors. They are usually single words like "heaven," "bell," "village chief," "king," etc. In some cases they involve abstract concepts like "covetous," "evil speaking," or "false creed."

Others have proposed that the inscriptions were meant as guides to aid pilgrims in their interpretation. This, however, does not account for the fact that in most cases the inscriptions were erased. The fact that some of them remain indicates that the construction of the new base covering the reliefs took place before all the inscriptions could be erased.

Outer Reliefs on the First Balustrade The new foot covering the reliefs provided a broad processional path along which pilgrims could walk to perform the meritorious *pradaksina* or ceremonial circumambulation around the stupa. This path had a low surrounding wall which has since disappeared.

While walking along this path, visitors can inspect the portraits of various magical beings—guardian monsters, forest nymphs, and *nagas* or water spirits associated with rivers and lakes. Also shown are humans flanked by women holding musical instruments, jewels, flowers, and fans. These do not symbolize any particular mythical beings, but were perhaps merely intended to reinforce the idea that when one enters the first gallery one begins to ascend the holy mountain and enters a realm populated by supernatural beings and forces.

Above: *This second panel (0.20) contrasts the serene life of a temperate family on the right with the unseemly behavior of dancers, drinkers and molesters on the left.*

Following pages: *A scene from the Rudrayana story in the* avadana *series on the main wall of the first gallery. The faithful minister Hiru arrives at his new home. This is one of Borobudur's most famous panels. The ship on the right is one of the best sources of information on ancient Indonesian ship construction. It is equipped with outriggers, like traditional Southeast Asian craft, and has several sails. The strong sensation of movement it imparts contrasts vividly with the serenity of the scene on the left, where the ship's passengers are greeted by a man and a woman who appear to live in the house in the background. The house is also realistically depicted in contrast to the rather fanciful structures found in other panels. The house's construction corresponds better to what we know of houses in other parts of Indonesia than to houses in Java. It is set on pillars and the roof employs the stressed ridge beam, like houses in the Minangkabau area of West Sumatra. (panel I.b86)*

The Jatakas and Avadanas
Previous Lives of the Buddhas

THE RELIEFS OF THE FIRST GALLERY WOULD HAVE been the first viewed by pilgrims as they circumambulated the monument. The pilgrim might even have chanted the stories aloud, just as Sumatran Buddhists did in the late seventh century according to the Chinese monk Yijing.

Jataka or "Birth Story" narratives depicting acts of self-sacrifice performed by Buddha in his earlier incarnations, and *avadanas* or "Heroic Deeds"—similar stories which differ from *jatakas* only in that the main character is not Buddha in an earlier incarnation—fill 500 panels on the balustrade of the first gallery and 120 panels on the main wall (beneath the *Lalitavistara*), and another 100 panels on the balustrade of the second gallery, making a total of 720 panels.

Borobudur illustrates quite a number of *jataka* and *avadana* stories in just a few panels. The stories can be compared to animal fables, fairytales, romances, and adventure stories. Some *avadanas* have very little religious significance and at least two stories even depict Buddha incarnated as a robber.

The upper series of reliefs on the first level balustrade are separated by decorative panels which have been criticized as being of poorer artistic quality compared to the panels on the rest of the monument. These were not in the original plan and were added later. Since the stones were not integrated into the structure but simply piled on the edge of the terrace, many have lost one or more pieces. The reason for this addition has not been discovered, but they probably were added to compensate for the loss of the *Mahakarmavibhangga* reliefs.

Few of the reliefs in this series have been identified.

The balustrade of the second gallery is also decorated with scenes illustrating *jataka* tales which are just as poorly understood as those on the first balustrade.

The Texts The first series of reliefs on the bottom row of the balustrade of the first terrace comes from a text known as the *Jatakamala* or "Garland of Birth Stories," written by a man named Aryasura in the fourth century. With the help of this text the first 34 stories (135 panels) have been identified.

Unfortunately only a small proportion of other panels in the *jataka-avadana* series have been deciphered and the majority remain "unreadable." Several ancient compilations of *jatakas* contained a total of 100 separate tales, and there is some indication that the Borobudur reliefs

Opposite: *Detail of a group of ladies-in-waiting. The kneeling one, second from left, carries a fly whisk made from an animal's tail casually over her shoulder.*

Below: *Detail from an* avadana *relief depicting the capture of the* kinnara *Manohara. All the* kinnaras *flee from the pond where they have been bathing, but Manohara, who is frozen by magic, is left behind. In the picture the* kinnaras *are shown flying above the lotus pond; one or two look back at Manohara, who stands unmoving. (panel I.b5)*

A scene from Story 8 in the Jatakamala *series. The future Buddha on horseback is attacked by a band of ogres, but is unharmed. (panel IB.b29)*

The Jatakamala "Birth Stories"

The variety and flavor of the Jatakamala *tales can best be perceived by giving short synopses of some of them. The stories essentially promote the notion of self-sacrifice. Numbers in parentheses refer to the lower series of relief panels on the first balustrade (IB.b), numbered consecutively from the east stairway and proceeding clockwise.*

Story 1 (panels 1-4): The future Buddha becomes a hermit in the mountains and meets a starving tigress, to whom he gives his body as food. As a result his remains are worshipped by the gods.

Story 2 (5-9): The future Buddha is a king. The god Indra comes in disguise as a blind man and Buddha gives him his eyes. Satisfied with his virtue, Indra returns them.

Story 3 (10-14): A man who gives food to four monks and a woman who gives food to one monk are reborn as a king and queen.

Story 4 (15-18): The future Buddha as head of a merchant guild. He and his wife take food to a monk, although to do so they have to pass over hell (shown as a cauldron with humans in it).

Story 5 (19-22): Reborn as a rich and highly charitable man, the future Buddha is tested by Indra, who steals his possessions. The future Buddha becomes a humble grass-cutter, but retains his generous nature and is rewarded.

Story 6 (23-25): The future Buddha is a rabbit who teaches his friends—a jackal, an otter and an ape—the importance of generosity. When Indra appears disguised as a brahman, his friends all bring food but the rabbit is unable to do so and jumps into the cooking fire himself.

Story 7 (26-28): The future Buddha is a rich man but becomes a hermit. As a reward for his charity to a brahman—Indra in disguise—he is granted his wish: food of the gods in order to feed the poor.

Story 8 (29-35): The future Buddha is born as a generous king named Maitribala. Forest ogres come to the kingdom but are unable to cause harm. They meet a cowherd (31) who tells them this is due to the king's virtue. The ogres ask the king for a human to eat. He has himself cut up and they are so struck they mend their ways.

Story 9 (36-39): The future Buddha born as generous Prince Visvangtara, son of King Sanjaya of the Sibi clan. A greedy neighboring king sends brahmans to ask for the prince's elephant, which he gives them. The clan exiles him for profligacy. Indra tests his resolve before rewarding him by having him taken back home. (39)

Story 10 (40-43): The future Buddha is once again a king. Brahmans in his court inform him that the only

depict approximately that many stories too. Examples of such collections are the *Avadanasataka*, literally "One Hundred *Avadanas*" and the *Divyavadana* or "Heavenly *Avadanas*." Such stories would have been in existence long before Buddhism's time. Their themes were later adapted to teach Buddhism's simplest concepts to less sophisticated devotees.

The order of stories on Borobudur after the first 34 does not correspond to any known collection. It is possible that Borobudur's builders did not refer only to a single source, but combined the *Jatakamala* with individual stories selected from a variety of sources. Perhaps some were never written down but were passed on orally

way to end a drought imperiling his kingdom is to hold great sacrifices. These would normally involve animals, but the king, taking pity on animals, tells his subjects that instead, evil-doers will be sacrificed. (41) All his people behave so well that none are sacrificed and the king distributes the money for the sacrifices among the poor.

Story 11 (44-47): The future Buddha is reborn as Indra. During a battle between the gods and demons the gods are in retreat, when Indra turns about to save some birds. The demons are thrown into confusion and flee.

Story 12: *Not depicted.*

Story 13 (48-52): The future Buddha is again a king. Brahmans advise him against marrying a beautiful married woman in his kingdom, for she will distract him. One day the king happens to see her and falls in love. Her husband offers to give her up, but the king refuses.

Story 14 (53-55): The future Buddha is an old and blind former ship's navigator, and merchants prevail upon him to accompany them on a voyage, for his presence was thought to bring good fortune. The ship is blown off course and comes to the entrance of hell. The future Buddha prays for salvation and the ship turns around. Rocks and sand brought up from the ocean bottom turn into gold and jewels, and they all return home wealthy.

Story 15 (56-57): The future Buddha as a fish prays for rain in a drought. The gods led by Indra take pity and bring water which they pour into the pool.

Story 16 (58): The future Buddha is a young quail who lives in a mountain forest and is weak since he eats no living beings. He stops a forest fire by praying to the fire god, who halts out of respect.

Story 17 (59-61): The future Buddha is Indra in the guise of a brahman who appears before a drunken king. He brings liquor to sell to the king as a pretext to teach him of the evils of this habit, which the king then gives up.

Story 18 (62-63): A simple story in which the future Buddha is born into a rich but generous family and renounces the world to live as a hermit.

A scene from Story 6: the future Buddha as a rabbit. When Indra (left) arrives disguised as a brahman, the rabbit's three friends—a jackal, an otter and an ape—all bring food. He is unable to do so, and instead jumps onto the fire himself (right). (panels IB.b24-25)[2]

Above: *A group of women in a pavilion. This jataka is so far unidentified, but the child is probably the bodhisattva, speaking to a rsi or teacher seated on the far right. (panel IIB.42)*

Opposite: *A scene from Story 3. The future Buddha and his wife once gave food to monks, and as a reward are reborn as king and queen. (panel IB.b10)*

Story 19 (64-68; 64 is missing): The future Buddha is again a hermit, accompanied by his six brothers and one sister. They live on lotus stems. Indra steals the future Buddha's portion as a test, which he of course passes and even rebukes Indra for interfering with his meditation.

Story 20 (69-71): The future Buddha is a royal treasurer. One day his mother-in-law visits his wife and the two believe that the treasurer has become a hermit. He hears of this, and although his wife and mother-in-law are grief-stricken, decides to become a hermit in reality.

Panel 72 is unidentified; it may belong to story 20 or 21.

Story 21 (73-76): The future Buddha is a rich, married brahman, but decides to become a hermit and his wife accompanies him. They meet a king who carries off the future Buddha's wife. He later sends her back out of fear

of the future Buddha's spiritual power.

Story 22 (77-80): The future Buddha is king of the swans, assisted by another named Sumukha. The future Buddha is captured by a hunter at a human king's request, but Sumukha refuses to leave him. The hunter is astounded by Sumukha's virtue and wishes to set them free, but they do not want to create trouble for the hunter. Therefore of their own accord they go to the king, who sets them on thrones.

Story 23 (81-85): The future Buddha is an ascetic named Mahabodhi who becomes the favorite of a king. The other courtiers, however, become jealous and cause the king to neglect him. The future Buddha debates with them and proves their doctrines erroneous, at which the king reinstates him as favorite.

The Avadanas "Heroic Deeds"

The Prince and the Nymph Manohara (panels I.b1-20): *This first narrative tells the story of Sudhana in over 20 panels found in the lower series on the main wall of the first gallery, beneath the Life of Buddha reliefs. The contents appear to follow a text called the* Divyavadana.

Sudhana is the crown prince of North Pancala, a prosperous land where the king, Sudhana's father, reigns benevolently. The king and queen are depicted holding court in a pavilion while ministers and priests sit outside under umbrellas and trees. (1) Two fans, one of peacock feathers and one of leaves, rise behind their heads. The building on the right is the palace and the niche in the center contains a conch used as a flower vase. The peaceful and harmonious kingdom attracts a *naga* "water spirit" who comes to live in a lake near the palace and causes the fields of the kingdom to be well-supplied with water.

The rival kingdom of South Pancala, on the other hand, is ruled by a harsh and tyrannical king, and the country is dry and poverty-stricken as a result. The king of South Pancala goes hunting and passes through many deserted villages. (2) His ministers tell him his conduct discourages any *naga* from blessing the realm.

The king offers to reward anyone who can bring a *naga* to his kingdom. A snake-charmer begins to weave a spell which will lure the *naga* from North Pancala in seven days. The *naga* feels the spell begin to take effect and in spite of his attempts is unable to resist. He would have been forced to go to the south against his will, but for the assistance of a hunter by the name of Halaka who lives beside the lake. (3)

In return for his help, the *naga* entertains Halaka and gives him a magical lariat which never fails to snare its prey. (4) The hunter uses it to capture a nymph named Manohara—a *kinnari* or half-human, half-bird creature (though in the reliefs she is always shown to be completely human) as she bathes in the lake. (5) Manohara gives him a jewel from her forehead, signifying that he has her completely in his power.

At that moment Prince Sudhana, who is on a hunting trip, happens by and the hunter offers the nymph to him. Sudhana immediately falls in love with her, accepts the hunter's offer, and rewards him handsomely. (6) He then marries her.

Two brahmans come to North Pancala. One becomes the king's chief priest, the other obtains Sudhana's promise that he will become chief priest upon Sudhana's ascent to the throne. The chief priest learns of this and

Above: *Detail from a relief depicting the Manohara story. Great rejoicing at the kinnara court as Sudhana and Manohara are reunited. (panel I.b19)*

Opposite: *Manohara escapes from the palace into the sky. The relief shows her accompanied by birds, soaring into the clouds. Her knees are bent in the position conventionally used to indicate flight. The haste of her ascent is beautifully suggested by the posture of her arms and hands. (panel I.b11)*

Above: *The story of the virtuous Sibi king,
who offers his own flesh to save a dove from
being eaten by a falcon, both of whom are
gods in disguise. Scales are shown weighing
the dove and the king's flesh. (panel I.b56)*

Opposite: *The Manohara story; Sudhana in
the kingdom of the nymphs. Sudhana sits on
the right, just about to place Manohara's ring
in a water jar. The other nymphs dip water
from the lotus pond and carry it into the
palace. (panel I.b16)*

seeks to eliminate Sudhana. He persuades the king to
send Sudhana to subdue a rebellious area which had
defeated seven previous attacks. (7)

Sudhana then gives Manohara's jewel to his mother
and asks her to guard his wife during his absence. (8)
Sudhana is shown in audience with his mother, the
Queen. In the relief he makes the gesture of respect to
her, signifying his request. The rest of the scene is occupied by courtiers holding fans, flowers, and regalia not
mentioned in the text.

Sudhana defeats the rebels through the aid of an army

of forest ogres. (9) That same night the king has a dream
which he asks his priest to interpret. The priest knows
that the true meaning is that Sudhana has triumphed, but
in another attempt to eliminate the prince he tells the
king that the dream betokens a disaster which can be
forestalled only if a *kinnari* is sacrificed. (10) The king
resists, but in the end accedes to the request.

The queen learns of the danger to Manohara and
allows her to escape by returning her jewel to her, whereupon Manohara immediately flies away. (11) She does not
wish to abandon her beloved prince, however, and so

Above and opposite: *The veneration of the virtuous king of the Sibi. In the relief, Indra has returned the flesh to the king, who is seated on a throne in the midst of courtiers and gods. The latter are not given specific marks of identification. (panel I.b57)*

stops at the home of a *rsi* who lives by the lake. She gives the wise man her ring and tells him how to find her in the country of the *kinnaras*.

Sudhana returns victorious, bringing much tribute to the king (12) and goes immediately to Manohara, but learns from his mother of her return to the court of her father, the *kinnara* king. (13, 14) Sudhana goes off in search of her and eventually comes to the dwelling of the *rsi,* who gives the prince the ring and tells him how to reach Manohara's kingdom. (15)

In the *kinnara* kingdom, Sudhana meets some nymphs drawing water which they tell him is to be used to wash the human odor from Princess Manohara. He drops her

ring into one of the water jars in the hope that she will find it. (16) Manohara recognizes the ring and finds a way to bring Sudhana into the palace.

Next she seeks her father's permission for him to remain with her. At first he threatens to kill Sudhana, but later relents and promises to allow him to stay if he can pass two tests. In the first Sudhana has to shoot an arrow through seven trees and hit a golden post. (17) In the second he has to identify Manohara from among a large group of nymphs. (18)

Sudhana passes both tests and the pair are reunited; a scene of great rejoicing then takes place at the *kinnara* court. (19) The couple are seated in the center (Manohara

has been defaced, unfortunately) with attendants, horses, and an elephant, who have no role in the story.

The solo dancer is isolated on this relief in one of the more unusual and effective compositions on Borobudur. Musicians are depicted in detail on the left. The chests beneath the throne with lotus flowers and leaves pouring out of it are not found in any other Borobudur relief and their significance here is unknown.

Eventually Sudhana and Manohara return together to Pancala where he is enthroned as king and they both live long and happy lives, always being generous and kind to their subjects. (20)

Panels 21-30 have not been identified.

Mandhatar, the Prince Whom Pride Nearly Destroyed. (panels I.b31-50) *Although this story has been identified with certainty as the inspiration for this series of panels, the reliefs deviate significantly from extant textual versions. Several reliefs refer to episodes which we do not possess in written form. The panels appear on the main wall of the first gallery, in the lower series.*

A king drinks fertility water meant for women and gives birth from his forehead to a son named Mandhatar. (31-38) When his father dies, Mandhatar becomes king. (39) One of his first acts is to banish some *rsis* who had cursed birds for disturbing their meditations. (40)

Mandhatar soon discovers that whatever he wishes for immediately comes true. First he makes a shower of grain fall so that his subjects no longer have to cultivate the soil. (41) Seeing that people have to spin, he causes thread to fall from heaven, and then noting that they still have to weave the thread into clothing, he asks for cloth which comes fluttering through the air. (42)

Mandhatar soon becomes proud and selfish. He makes gold fall for seven days, but only into his own chamber. (43) Mandhatar's next thought is nothing less than to conquer the earth, and in that too, he is successful. (44)

Finally he asks his minister what remains to be accomplished, and is told that only the heavens of the gods are

Opposite: *A detail from the Rudrayana story, showing courtiers seated before the king in the royal pavilion at Rajagrha. (panel I.b77)*

Left: *The final scene from the Maitrakanyaka story, in which he is condemned to receive the same punishment as the man at right: to have his head torn by an iron wheel for 66,000 years. (panel I.b112)*

outside his control.

The god Indra then gives Mandhatar suzerainty over half the kingdom of the gods, (46) and Mandhatar even succeeds in bringing victory to them in a war against the demons, (47) whereupon he conceives the idea of becoming sole ruler of the gods. (48,49)

Miraculous retribution follows immediately, however. He falls from heaven and after confessing that he now realizes he had not obtained satisfaction from all his feats, he dies. (50)

Panels 51-55 have not been identified.

Indra and the Virtuous Sibi King. (panels I.b56-57)
Indra, king of the gods, frequently appears to subject reputedly virtuous men to various trials.

Indra disguises himself as a falcon and chases a dove, causing it to flee to the Sibi king for protection. The falcon protests that he will die if he is not allowed to eat the dove. The king offers his own flesh equal to the weight of the dove, but no matter how much he adds to the balance it never tips the scale. (56) Finally he puts his entire body on the balance. Indra then acknowledges the king's virtue and makes him whole once more. (57)

Above: *Unidentified scene of children playing in a rive, with nursemaids watching over them. The children are recoiling from menacing figures, perhaps yaksas, approaching from the right. One makes a menacing gesture toward the children and women. Another child on the far left gestures toward the upstream part of the river. (panel I.b95)*

Opposite: *The Manohara story; rejoicing in the kinnara court as Sudhana and the nymph are reunited. The relief shows a dancer with musicians seated to the left. (panel I.b19)*

Previous pages: *The merchant Maitraka-nyaka greeted by sixteen nymphs (here represented by eleven). Each time he moves to a new city, more* apsaras *come out to greet him. (panel I.b110)*

Above: *Maitrakanyaka's shipwreck and his arrival at the city of nymphs. On the right are men abandoning the ship. A sea monster is about to sink it and men climb aboard a lifeboat. The tree at the left separates this scene from the subsequent episode, in shadow-play fashion. (panel I.b108)*

Opposite: *Detail from an unidentified story. A group of men, perhaps deities, look on as a nobleman lets fly an arrow. (panel Ib.119)*

The Testing of a Prince (panels I.b58-60) *A story very similar to that of the Sibi king.*

The Virtuous Queen (panels I.b61-63) A princess follows her leprous spouse into exile. Her virtue attracts Indra's attention. He heals the prince and they return to the palace.

King Rudrayana and His Queen, and the Fate of the Evil Prince. (panels I.b64-88) Rudrayana is a virtuous king. Some visiting merchants from Rajagrha, where Buddha was then living, tell him that they are ruled over by a virtuous king named Bimbisara. (64) Rudrayana sends Bimbisara a letter (65,66) and valuable jewels (67); Bimbisara responds with a chest of rare garments. (68) Rudrayana then sends him an even more precious gift—a bejeweled cuirass. (69) Bimbisara reciprocates by sending the most valuable object he can think of—a painting of Buddha. (70)

Rudrayana wishes to learn about Buddha and asks Bimbisara to send him a monk. (71,72) When the palace women ask for instruction, a nun arrives (73) and so impresses the queen that she, too, becomes a nun. (74) She attains such virtue that she becomes a spirit.

The queen then appears to the king (75) and asks him to become a monk so that they can be reunited in heaven. Rudrayana abdicates in favor of his son (76) and goes to Rajagrha, where Buddha ordains him as a monk. One day while begging, he meets King Bimbisara, who tries to convince Rudrayana to become king again, but he remains firm in his resolve. (77)

The son who has replaced him, Sikhandin, becomes a tyrant. Rudrayana learns of this, again from merchants, and decides to return to correct his son. Sikhandin sends men to waylay and kill his father. When they meet him on the road he asks permission to meditate, becomes a spirit like his wife, (78) and allows himself to be killed.

Sikandin begins to repent of his crime but evil coun-

selors prevent him from reforming. (80) He nearly buries alive the monk who had converted his father, but his father's former ministers intervene in time to save him. (81) The monk informs them that for six days gold and jewels will fall from the sky, but on the seventh a great sandstorm will bury the city. The ministers collect valuable objects and escape by ship to found new cities. (82)

As the sandstorm begins, the monk leaves the city accompanied by a minister's son. They visit another city where he leaves behind his bowl, which the people honor as a relic, building a stupa over it and holding regular celebrations for it. (83) They come to another city where the people ask the minister's son to remain as their king. (84) At a third city the monk leaves his staff, where another stupa is erected for it. (85)

The main characters arrive at their new homes. A minister named Hiru goes to Hiruka (86), the monk to Sravasti (87), the other minister Bhiru to Bhirukaccha. (88)

Bhallatiya and the Kinnara (panels I.b89-91) While hunting in the Himalayas, the king of Benares sees a *kinnara* couple embracing and weeping. (89) They tell him that they were once separated for a single night by a flooded river. *Kinnaras* live for a thousand years and this happened 697 years earlier, but they still regretted that one lost night. (90) The king returns to his palace and tells the story to his court.

Panels 91-105 have not been identified.

The Story of Maitrakanyaka. (panels I.b106-112) A merchant of Benares dies on a voyage shortly after the birth of his son Maitrakanyaka. When Maitrakanyaka becomes a man he asks his mother how his father had been employed, so that he too can engage in the same occupation. Not wanting him to take dangerous trips abroad, she tells him that his father had owned a shop. He then gives his mother the four coins he earns on his first day of work at a shop, to distribute to the poor.

In a scene from an unidentified story, a king (or bodhisattva?) holds a lotus stem in his left hand while seated on a throne supported by a lion. Male attendants sit on his right, females on his left. (panel I.b113)

Upon being told that his father had been a perfume dealer, Maitrakanyaka changes to that trade and immediately makes eight coins, which he again gives his mother to give away. (106) Next he hears that his father had been a goldsmith, so he adopts that trade and makes first 16, then 32 coins in profit. Jealous of his success, the other merchants tell him of his father's true profession, whereupon he determines to set off on a trading expedition. His mother begs him not to go but he rudely kicks her aside and departs. (107)

Maitrakanyaka's ship sinks, but he manages to reach shore and finds his way to a city where four nymphs greet him. He lives there luxuriously for some time, (108) but wishing to travel again he goes to another city where eight nymphs greet him. (109) After several more years he goes to another city where no fewer than 16 nymphs

receive him. (110) This is repeated yet again, with 32 nymphs springing up at the gates of the next city. (111)

Maitrakanyaka eventually leaves this city for yet another, but this proves to be his undoing for when he reaches the gates no nymphs greet him. Instead he comes upon a man whose head is being torn apart constantly by an iron wheel (112) as punishment for mistreating his mother. Instantly the wheel flies from the man's head and begins to torture Maitrakanyaka.

Maitrakanyaka is told that his punishment will last 66,000 years, after which another man will come to receive the same torment. Maitrakanyaka, however, offers to wear the wheel forever to spare others the same pain, and is immediately freed from the punishment and reborn in the Heaven of Contentment.

Panels 113-120 have not been identified.

Above: *In the sequel to the panel on pages 90-91, the chief figure (probably the same one who occupied the lion throne) sets off on horseback into a forest, accompanied by men prepared for hunting, as their arrows attest. The forest at left is thick with many sorts of game. (panel I.b114)*

Opposite: *In this rather poorly preserved scene from an unidentified tale, moustached warriors holding swords sit before a bodhisattva on a throne. (panel I.b115)*

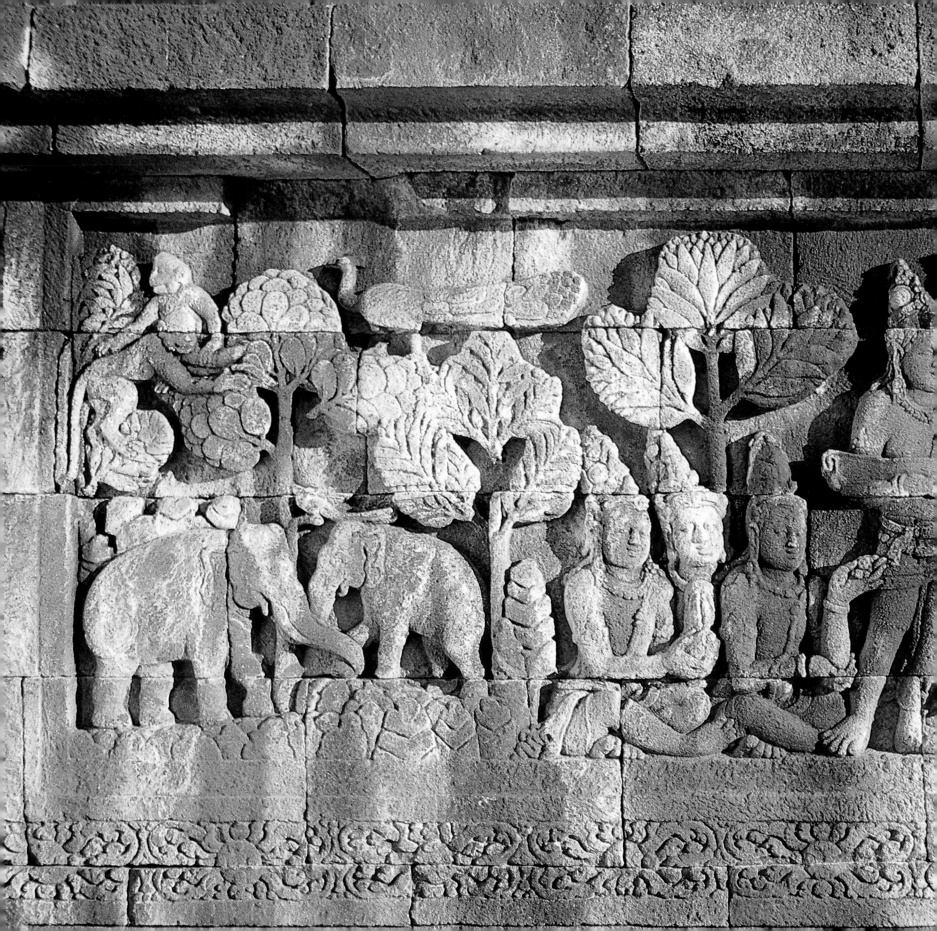

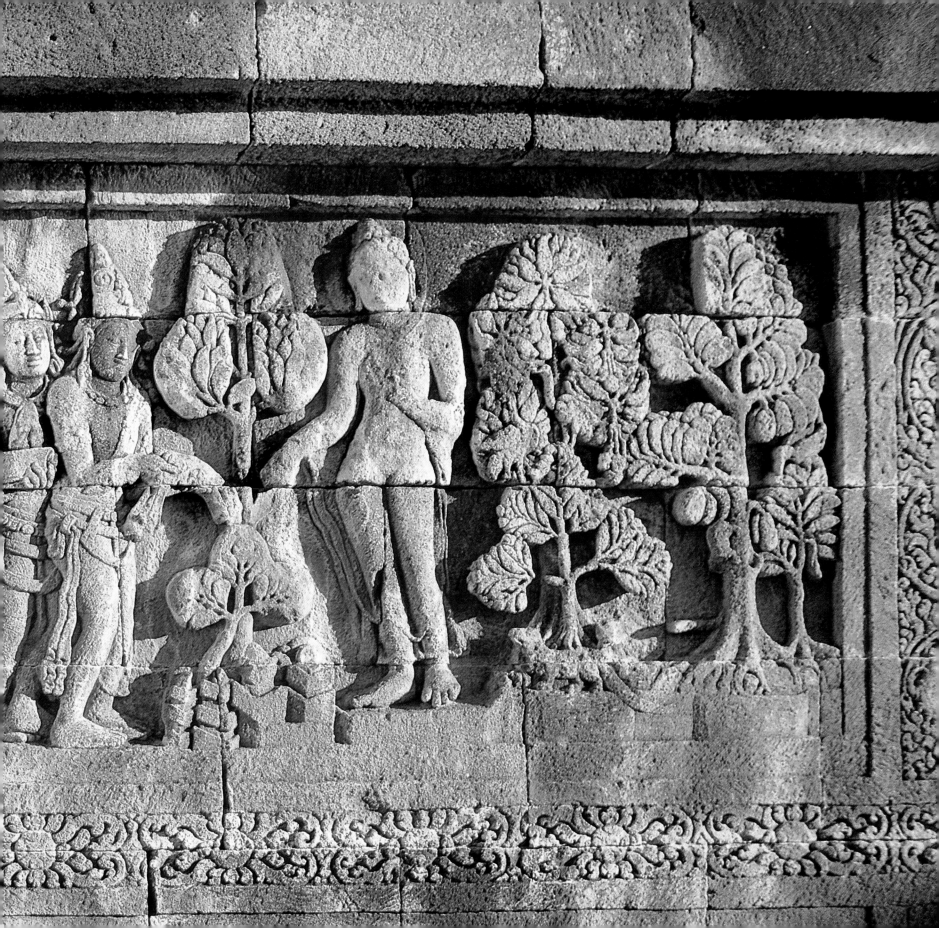

The Lalitavistara
Life of Gautama Buddha

ALL APPROACHES TO BOROBUDUR LOOK THE same. Only when scholars began to identify the narrative reliefs did they discover that the main entrance lay to the east, for the stories begin there and proceed clockwise around the galleries. This suggests that visitors were meant to approach Borobudur from this direction, stopping first at Mendut and Pawon as part of the same pilgrimage route.

Those entering the monument climb the eastern stairway to the first gallery and turn left to begin their journey, so that the monument is always to their right. To view the relief panels in sequence, visitors walk clockwise around the monument, performing a ceremonial circumambulation which produces spiritual merit.

We do not know the precise place where devotees would have begun their instruction. Visitors to the first gallery see four series of reliefs—two on either side of the gallery, an upper and a lower one. As we have seen, three of these are devoted to the *jataka* and *avadana* tales. The most prominent set of panels, however—the upper series to which one's attention is naturally drawn as one enters the first gallery—illustrates a Buddhist story well-known throughout the world: the life of the historical Buddha, Sakyamuni or Siddharta Gautama.

The life of Buddha reliefs cover the upper half of the main wall all around the first gallery of the monument, a total of 120 panels. The reliefs were carved to illustrate a text entitled the *Lalitavistara*, "The Unfolding of the Play." This title refers to the idea that Buddha's last incarnation was a performance intentionally given to enlighten mankind before he vanished from existence. The reliefs of Borobudur are the most elaborate depiction of this drama on any monument in the world.

The life story of Buddha series, however, is not the longest on Borobudur. More panels are devoted to the story of Sudhana which fills the second, third and fourth galleries. This is not surprising, since for the Buddhist believer, Sakyamuni was only the last incarnation of a being whose previous existences are traced in hundreds of panels depicting the *jataka* tales on the balustrades of the first and second galleries.

The Text Several basic versions of Gautama Buddha's life were widespread in ancient Asia, but none was written down until several centuries after Gautama's death. The *Buddhacarita*, "The Acts of Buddha," exists in two versions. The one attributed to Sangharaksa, who lived in India around 2,000 years ago, has been preseved in a Chinese translation. The other is said to have been written in the second century A.D. by Asvaghosha. The *Buddhacarita* recounts all the important events in Buddha's life until he attains Nirvana.

The version of the *Lalitavistara* which Borobudur's designers chose to follow is shorter and reaches its conclusion with the sermon in the Deer Park at Benares. The forty more years he spent wandering and teaching before he concluded his final incarnation are disregarded. The reason for this neglect, which may seem surprising to some, is that Mahayana Buddhism believed that the preaching of the First Sermon was the climax of all of Gautama's previous existences, including those depicted in the *jatakas*. Once he had accomplished this, the next logical step was to demonstrate the implications of this sermon for the pilgrim. This is fulfilled by the *Gandavyuha* reliefs on the upper galleries.

Opposite: *After his enlightenment Gautama Buddha sets off for Benares to preach his first sermon. On the way he is stopped in several towns, whose inhabitants come to honor him. Here the citizens of a city bring him offerings. (panel 109)*

Previous pages: *Gautama receives his monk's robe, offered by a god. The six gods are depicted without any special marks of identification. The peacocks, monkeys and elephants on the far left are the artist's own elaborations. (panel 83)*

Above: *Sakyamuni in the Heaven of Contentment. The relief interprets the text by portraying drummers floating on clouds. The first one to the right of the palace has his legs bent beneath him, a convention used by the Borobudur sculptors to show that he is flying. Nymphs are also portrayed. The first nymph on the left holds an incense burner. (panel 1)*

Opposite: *A detail from the panel above, showing the celestial musicians in the Heaven of Contentment. (panel 1)*

Gautama was not a real person, but only an identity assumed by a boddhisattva in order to fulfill his duty to help other beings attain liberation. What happened to him later was therefore inconsequential. Borobudur was not a monument for the worship of Gautama, but an instrument to teach people how to become bodhisattvas, as well as a place where they could be assisted to achieve that goal. Gautama was only one example, although a primary one, of how others had attained Nirvana.

The *Lalitavistara* text which Borobudur's designers followed was slightly different from any now known, but these differences are matters of detail. Some of the same scenes are depicted on Buddhist monuments in India, and in a few instances the Borobudur panels are similar to those found elsewhere, showing that the Javanese were familiar with the conventional designs for these scenes. In most cases, however, they did not follow those conventions but created their own original scenes.

The Reliefs As a group, the panels on the first gallery are fortunately among the best-preserved on the monument, except for some on the south wall. The protective blanket of soil which the centuries laid over parts of the monument was probably deepest in the first gallery. However, since the south face of the edifice gets direct sunlight for only a few months a year, it remains damper and provides the best environment for moss and lichen which damage the stone.

The text did not give the artists much direction, for it is in prose and often highly abstract. Those who compare the text and the reliefs come to appreciate the achievement of the monument's designers and sculptors in transforming complicated descriptions and philosophical concepts into compositions whose rhythm and grace are musical in nature. Certainly the sculptors were familiar with musical instruments and dance movements, and it is probable that these arts played as important a role in ancient Java as they do today. One wonders whether the notes of the Javanese *gamelan* could be heard softly as pilgrims slowly made their way around the monument.

'The Unfolding of the Play'

Episode 1: The Prelude to the Birth of Buddha. *Panels 1-15, leading from the eastern stairway of the first gallery to the southeast corner. Numbers in parentheses indicate the panel on Borobudur which corresponds to the text. It begins by describing the future Buddha in the Heaven of Contentment, which is one of the levels of paradise in Mahayana Buddhism. He is not yet Buddha but a bodhisattva; in order to distinguish him from other buddhas found in later reliefs, we shall call him Sakyamuni.*

The Heaven of Contentment floats among the clouds above Indra's palace on the peak of Mt. Sumeru. The future Buddha lives here in a palace filled with the perfume of flowers and music made from millions of instruments while almost incalculable numbers of gods adore and praise him. (1) The future Buddha informs the gods that he has decided to be reborn on earth. (2) A cord around his waist supports his right knee, a convention used in Borobudur to denote people of high status. The cord or *yogapatta* was used to help the wearer stay for long periods in a meditative pose called *ardhaparyangka*, in which the left knee is raised, left heel on the ground, right leg down and the right heel against the groin.

In honor of Gautama's approaching birth, some gods descend to earth to teach brahmans. (3) The two damaged figures in the upper right corner of the relief probably represent gods during their descent. On the left a god in the guise of a brahman—typified by his moustache, beard, bun hairdo and simple attire—is giving a lesson.

Another god goes to the Deer Park at Benares, near Buddha's future earthly home, to tell a group of *pratyeka* buddhas[4] that Buddha will soon come to earth. He asks them to give up existence in deference to Buddha. They rise into the air and enter Nirvana. (4) In the relief the figure on the right has already begun to ascend.

Buddha teaches the "Introduction of the Law" to the gods (5) and gives his crown to a bodhisattva named Maitreya, whom he designates his successor as the next Buddha. (6) He then asks the gods what form he should take when he descends from heaven into his mother's womb. (7) Some suggest that he go in human form, but one who had been a *rsi* or wise man in a former life announces that the brahmans' books described the future Buddha as descending in the form of "the mighty shape of a splendid elephant with six tusks, as if enclosed in a golden net, brightly shining, with a head red and most beautiful with the sap that oozes from its forehead."[5]

Queen Maya and King Suddhodana, Sakyamuni's future mother and father, live in a palace in the city of Kapilavastu. (8) The king grants queen Maya her request to undertake a vow of self-denial. Some goddesses go to Kapilavastu to see the woman who is worthy of being Sakyamuni's mother. (9) Queen Maya is seated in her quarters with her attendants in waiting. The central action of the episode is the descent of the goddesses who are curious to see Buddha's future mother. They are represented by the two celestial women in the upper left corner of the panel.

The gods discuss which of them should accompany Buddha on his descent to earth. (10) In the relief, the gods are seated in a pavilion which seems to be a faithful representation of a Javanese *pendopo* with carved wooden pillars and a highly-decorated roof with a *kala* head on the beam. On the right is a temple-like building with rampant lions very similar to those at Candi Ngawen, in the southeast part of Kedu.

Other bodhisattvas come to pay homage to Buddha

Queen Maya and King Suddhodhana in the palace of Kapilavastu. The queen has come to ask permission to take a vow of self-denial. The king and queen are shown in a garden pavilion, symbolized by trees nearby. The king's gesture signifies his consent to her request. The text says that the queen came with 10,000 women. In the relief they are represented by the five women behind the queen. The guards and servants to the left and right are not mentioned in the text. (panel 8)

just before he descends to earth. (11) During the "Great Descent" Buddha sits on his throne in a pavilion, accompanied by uncountable numbers of gods, nymphs and other supernatural beings. (12)

Buddha, in the shape of the elephant in the upper left corner of the relief, enters Queen Maya's womb while she sleeps. That night a lotus grows from the ocean until it reaches Brahma's heaven. The lotus contains the essence of all creation. Brahma collects the essence in a bowl made of lapis lazuli, and as a mark of honor gives Buddha the essence to drink. (13) This is one of the most popular scenes in ancient Buddhist art. It is depicted in a similar manner on many Indian monuments, suggesting that Borobudur's designers were aware of the convention according to which this scene was normally rendered.

Sakyamuni, in a magical pavilion inside his mother's womb, receives visits from gods and explains the Law to them. His hand is in *vitarka mudra*, symbolizing the preaching of the Law. (14)

Queen Maya decides to go to a forest of *asoka* trees. When she arrives she sends a servant to ask the king to meet her there. (15) In the relief the queen is standing with one hand outstretched to a kneeling servant, probably in the act of instructing her to go to the king. The palace which she has left is portrayed in great detail on the right half of the scene. It resembles a Javanese temple more than a palace, with *kala* and *makara* ornaments by the door, and towers on the corners of the roof. The motif on the pinnacle is a *vajra*, emblem of the Diamond World, a symbol of great significance in Javanese Bud-

dhism. No such pinnacle motifs have been found on temple sites, so we cannot tell whether they actually were used or whether this is an artist's imaginary temple.

Episode 2: The Birth and Early Life of Buddha. *Panels 16-45, on the southern side of the monument.*

When the king arrives at the edge of the forest he is suddenly unable to go any further. Some gods inform him of the reason: the queen is pregnant with the future Buddha. (16) In the relief the king is shown standing outside the gate to the pavilion where the queen awaits, represented by the small structure in the center. The roof of the queen's pavilion is adorned with more *vajra* motifs. The scene takes place in the forest, but trees are not illustrated. Instead the relief depicts the king's elephant on the left, although this is not mentioned in extant versions of the text. The elephant, like the umbrella, was a symbol of royalty in ancient Java.

The king is able to approach the queen, who informs him of her dream, in which an elephant entered her womb. She asks him to send for brahmans to interpret the dream. (17) In the relief the queen holds her hands in a gesture of supplication, while the king's hands indicate his approval of her request.

The brahmans tell the royal couple that the queen will bear a son who will either become a universal ruler or a buddha. (18) The brahmans are identifiable by their hairdo and beards, in particular one who is seated on a raised seat. The king and queen are satisfied with the prophesy and give the brahmans garments and other gifts. (19)

Indra and other gods offer their palaces for the queen to live in during her pregnancy. (20) In the relief no particular gods can be identified by name. They face the king, who sits on the right inside a very ornate pavilion. The gods, as well as the king himself, build various palaces for Queen Maya.

To prevent any of the gods or the king from being disappointed, the unborn Sakyamuni creates the illusion that Queen Maya is in each of the palaces. (21) In the relief three palaces are shown, with Queen Maya in each of them. Standing beside them are four goddesses who come

to serve Sakyamuni. Note again the *vajra* roof motifs.

During her pregnancy the queen acquires certain powers: the power to restore people possessed by supernatural beings to their normal state by letting them view her, and the power to heal diseases by placing her right hand on their heads or letting them grasp a sheaf of grass which she holds. (22) In the relief the queen extends her hand toward a man dressed as a noble. He holds his sore arm, while behind him more commoners await her healing touch. There is a gateway behind the queen.

The Sakya tribe celebrate the approaching birth by

Queen Maya sits in a pavilion, surrounded by many serving women. She has just been chosen to be the bodhisattva's future mother. (panel 9)

Above and opposite: *The Great Descent of Sakyamuni. Seated on his throne in a pavilion (shown opposite), Sakyamuni is carried by gods, nymphs, and other supernatural beings. The supporters all have their legs upraised and beneath the throne the clouds of the sky can be seen. Attendants hold parasols, important symbols of high status in ancient Java (shown above, in a detail from the left side of the panel). Parasols were of many varieties and denoted social standing. Streamers and pennants flutter in the wind, emphasizing swift movement through the air. (panel 12)*

distributing gifts to the poor. (23) In the relief the king stands on the far right in front of a building with a distinctive profile, probably representing a contemporary, two-storied Javanese structure built of wood. Such buildings are unknown in modern Java, but structures of quite similar form are still found in Nepal. They are called *sat-tal*, a word deriving from the Sanskrit term for "alms-house," and are pavilions of one or more stories with a portion of the interior set aside for ascetics who wish to remain in the building for some time. A part of the building is also used as a religious shrine.[6]

The king lives as a hermit during the queen's pregnancy. (24) The damaged portion on the right of the relief probably represents the king. The activities of the many

other people in the scene are not explained by the extant texts. The Javanese version may have added some details which are now lost.

Various portents appear as the time of the prince's birth approaches. Lion cubs descend from the Himalayas, perform circumambulations of the city and lie down peacefully at the gates. Baby elephants come to touch the king's feet with their trunks. Young gods appear in the king's chamber and sit on his lap and those of others in the room. (25)

Queen Maya asks the king to be allowed to give birth in the Lumbini Pleasure Garden.[7] (26) She is seated on the right of the relief and the king is in the center, completely obliterated.

Sakyamuni enters Queen Maya's womb in the form of an elephant. The queen is asleep inside her palace, which is elaborately depicted, while her maids fan and caress her. Lesser servants gather beneath the house.

Queen Maya sets off in a carriage for the park, accompanied by a huge retinue. The text mentions 84,000 horse carriages and similarly large numbers of elephant carriages, warriors, women, musicians, goddesses, and other supernatural beings. (27)

When the queen arrives at the Lumbini Garden she walks until she comes to a tree which magically bends down before her. She grasps a limb, and Sakyamuni comes out of her right side. The baby miraculously takes seven steps in each of the four compass directions and at each step a lotus springs up. (28) In the relief the queen still grasps the branch while maids wash her feet, and the newborn prince (sadly much defaced) takes seven steps that are marked by lotuses.

After Sakyamuni's birth, *rsis* come to congratulate King Suddhodhana. Indra and Brahma disguise themselves as brahmans and also take part. (29) The relief presents two main figures: the king on the right and a *rsi* on the left in a pavilion. To the left are brahmans being treated to a feast.

A week after Sakyamuni is born, Queen Maya dies and becomes a goddess. Her sister Gautami becomes the baby prince's guardian. (30) The relief illustrates this episode by showing the child on Gautami's lap, surrounded by servants and nursemaids.

Another great *rsi* named Asita who lives in the Himalayas sees portents of Sakyamuni's birth, and with his nephew flies to Kapilavastu to see the child. (31) In the panel, the *rsi* and his nephew are on the left while Prince Sakyamuni sits on his father's lap. The prince is depicted in the next few panels with unusual consistency: seated with legs wide apart, a crescent-shaped motif behind his head. In the center of the panel, palace attendants bring gifts of garments for the *rsis*. The elephant and horses are not mentioned in our versions of the text.

More gods, led by Siva, come to pay respect to the prince. (32) In the relief Siva is probably the third figure from the left, with his hands clasped in the position denoting worshipful respect. The space to the right is filled with detailed depictions of guards with shields, bows, and arrows not mentioned in extant texts and probably added by the sculptor.

The elder members of the Sakya tribe suggest that the child should be taken to the temple. (33) The king inclines his head in assent. The figures bearing various objects such as a fly whisk are probably the sculptor's additions. The king and Sakyamuni, together with a large retinue including brahmans, guards, religious teachers and others set off for the temple. (34) The charioteer is depicted as a dwarf, vigorously tugging at the reins.

When the prince arrives, the statues in the temple, including Siva, Kuvera, Candra, Surya, Indra, Brahma, and others come to life and kneel before him. (35) In the relief, the procession has arrived at the temple, which is portrayed in detail. It does not correspond precisely to any known archaeological remains; it has two stories and a projecting roof supported by pillars. On the pinnacle is a *cakra*, the symbol of Visnu. The statues in the temple are shown as four large figures beside the temple. The one standing may be Brahma, but the others have not been given identifying characteristics. Another god is just coming out of the door. The prince stands in front of his father wearing a low crown of the type worn by children.

The king has five hundred ornaments of gold and other jewels made for the prince. When the prince puts them on they lose all their brightness in comparison with his own radiance. Vimala, who is the goddess of the park, appears and explains the miracle to the king. (36) The relief shows Sakyamuni in a pavilion on the right, seated with one leg down, while courtiers bring the ornaments to him. Vimala is also shown in the left part of the panel

talking to the seated king.

When Sakyamuni comes of the proper age he is sent to school. The schoolmaster, Visvamitra, is overcome by the prince's appearance and faints. A god named Subhangga helps him up with his right hand. (37) The relief shows the prince and his father in the center, sheltered by a parasol, with Visvamitra kneeling before them. Behind him, inside a palisade, is the school. This style of building no longer exists in Java, but its close relatives are found in the houses of Sumatra and Sulawesi. On the far right the schoolmaster is lying down, overcome by the prince's

In honor of the bodhisattva's approaching birth, the Sakya distribute alms to the people. Here a royal figure, perhaps the king himself with his high crown, gives food to bearded rsis (wise men) and others. (panel 23)

Queen Maya's procession to the Lumbini Pleasure Garden. The queen is shown escorted by members of the Sakya tribe. The sculptors mark the movement of people by tilting the parasols and standards. (panel 27)

appearance, while Subhangga helps him up. Unfortunately this section of the relief is badly damaged.

The next episode recounts the beginning of the prince's education. (38) The prince, his knee supported in a sling, sits in a pavilion with Visvamitra on his right. Although bearded in the previous scene, here Visvamitra is beardless, an example of the variability in the portrayal of the same character by different sculptors. Other pupils sit in another pavilion on the left, holding palm leaf scrolls.

The story now skips some years ahead. The prince decides to visit a rural village. (39) The relief depicts him undertaking the trip in a carriage, although this is not specified by the texts we possess. In the countryside the prince sits down under a guava tree to meditate. Five *rsis* who happen to be flying through the air nearby are obstructed by an invisible force, which the local guardian spirit tells them is the prince. In India this scene of the first meditation is often portrayed with a farmer and plow in the background, a convention not followed on Borobudur. The five *rsis* are shown paying homage to Sakyamuni. (40)

The king, reminded by members of the tribe of the prophesy that his son is to become either a buddha or a great ruler, and wishing that the prince succeed him as king, decides to ask Sakyamuni to marry. The prince says he will give his answer in seven days. (41)

The prince consents to take a wife and chooses Gopa. Only she among all young women can bear to look at him without being blinded by his radiance. The prince gives her a ring from his finger. (42) The relief shows him

doing so; the peacocks on the roof perhaps symbolize the coming marriage.

Gopa's father is not convinced of the prince's suitability as a suitor for his daughter, and so requires the prince to undergo some tests to prove his mental and physical prowess, never before demonstrated. The prince tells his father he consents to be tested. (43)

A rival Sakya prince, Devadatta, encounters a white elephant being brought into town for Sakyamuni, and out of jealousy kills it with a blow of his fist. (44) Sakyamuni sees the dead elephant lying by the city gate. He throws the elephant over seven walls and seven moats of the city so that its rotting carcass will not disturb the citizens. (45) Little of this relief remains aside from the prince's guards.

Episode 3: Buddha's Marriage and Renunciation of His Earlier Life. *Panels 46-75, on the western side.*

Sakyamuni, along with five hundred other princes, goes out of the city to demonstrate his powers. He sets a problem which no other prince but he can solve. (46) In the relief King Suddhodhana sits on the far right and Sakyamuni is in the center explaining the solution.

The next two panels on Borobudur depict parts of the competition which are not found in extant versions of the *Lalitavistara*. First the Sakya princes are shown in a pavilion on the left. Sakyamuni stands in the center holding the stem of a lotus, and the king sits on the right. (47) In the next panel Sakyamuni still stands in the same pose, while the king on the right makes a gesture as if in congratulation. (48) Without an explanatory text, no sense can be made of these two scenes.

The next test is an archery competition. Sakyamuni uses an ancient bow which had been preserved in a temple since his grandfather's time; no one else could even bend it. He sends an arrow through the seven trees shown on the panel, and through various other targets including an iron boar. (49)

Gopa's father agrees to the marriage. The palace courtiers criticize her for immodesty because she does not cover her face with a veil. Gopa defends herself, saying

Sakyamuni introduces Gopa to the other women in the palace. Sakyamuni is shown seated on a throne with his left leg supported by a sling, a common attribute of royalty meant to help them sit more comfortably, while women admire him. (panel 51)

The Great Departure. This scene is represented in many other Buddhist sculptures, but the Borobudur composition does not resemble them. The prince is shown making his escape on his horse Kanthaka, whose feet are supported by gods so that he will not make any sound to arouse the guards. The two figures leading the way are the gods Indra and Brahma. The lines which emanate from the tree on the right are reflections from the brightness of the prince's body in the darkness of night. (panel 65)

that immodest people are those who are not virtuous and truthful, while those who have self-control are virtuous whether or not they cover their faces. The king approves of her response and gives her presents. (50)

The prince goes to the quarters of his women and declares Gopa to be his chief wife. (51) Sakyamuni sits on a throne while women admire him and Gopa, leaning against a servant, faces other women seated in a palace.

Various gods, including Indra and Brahma and other supernatural beings, congratulate the prince on his marriage and ask him when he will begin his quest for enlightenment. (52) In the relief the prince is seated in a pavilion with one leg down. Between the prince and gateway on the far right are female musicians. The gods, in

supplicating postures, are shown on the left of the pavilion. Various guards and supernatural beings are present behind them.

At first the prince makes no response. A god named Hrideva comes to the prince in the middle of the night and advises him to leave. (53) In the relief the prince is seated in a palace surrounded by a palisade. Behind him women slump in sleep, while gods descend on clouds to speak to him. Outside the gate many guards also drowse.

The king dreams of the prince's departure and tries to attract him to remain by building three more palaces to amuse him. (54)

The king also posts guards around the prince's palace and sends many young women to entertain him. (55)

This is one of the most successful compositions on the monument. On the right the prince is soothed by two women; on the left Gopa is composing her hair while gazing at herself in a mirror. In the center is the facade of the third palace. The three men standing in front of the gateway and the elephant and rider are not mentioned in extant texts.

One day the prince decides to visit a royal pleasure garden. On the way, as the result both of his own power and that of the gods, an old man suddenly appears to him. The prince returns to his palace without reaching the garden. This is the first of the Four Encounters which motivate the prince to undertake his arduous quest for enlightenment. (56)

In the second of the Four Encounters the prince again sets out for his pleasure garden, but on the way, again through divine intervention, he sees a sick man. (57) The apparition is again shown on the far left, the gods on the right, and the clouds above.

On another occasion the prince sees a dead man surrounded by grieving relatives. (58) In the relief the dead man is again placed on the far left beneath a roof which is not specified by the text and may depict an ancient Javanese funerary structure. The carriage depicted in this scene is the most elaborate one on the temple, with a highly decorated shaft terminating in a lion. The gods on the far right of the panel have been badly damaged, although they were still visible according to a drawing of

Above: *Sakyamuni has left the palace and dismissed his horse and groom. Henceforth he wanders on foot. Sakyamuni stands at the left beneath a parasol, bidding farewell to the supernatural beings who accompanied him during his Great Departure. (panel 66)*

Opposite: *Sakyamuni has come to the palace to ask his father's permission to leave. The sleeping courtiers indicate that it is the middle of the night. (panel 61)*

the relief made in the 1850s.

The fourth encounter, again contrived by the gods, involves a monk. He is at peace, in contrast to the grief and suffering felt by the others, who are still at the mercy of their own uncontrollable desires. The prince meditates on the example of the monk and on the path to salvation from suffering. (59)

That night he comforts Gopa who has a bad dream. (60) It is difficult to discern if this episode is actually the one depicted in this relief, since the prince is shown sitting alone in his palace.

Sakyamuni then goes to the king and is granted permission to leave. (61) The prince sits on his father's right in the king's palace. The sleeping courtiers indicate that it is the middle of the night. The king's gesture is one of granting a request.

The rest of the Sakya tribe wish to prevent Sakyamuni from leaving, and Gautami asks all the women to surround the prince. (62) The prince is illustrated seated in a pavilion decorated with a *kala-makara* motif surrounded by a palisade, with many women crowding around him.

The gods, however, cause the women's quarters to look ugly and in disarray, while the women look unkempt and sleep in awkward and disgusting postures, even snoring. (63) These apparitions serve to remind the prince that the human body is a decaying prison for the spirit and increases his desire to escape and begin his journey toward enlightenment.

The prince goes out of the palace and calls for his horse Kanthaka. (64) With the assistance of the gods the prince then makes his Great Departure, leaving his former life behind forever. (65)

When the prince has left the kingdom of the Sakyas behind, he descends from Kanthaka and says goodbye to the gods and other supernatural beings who have escorted him. (66) These include *yaksas*, the figures on the far right with moustaches and coarse features. The sculptor of this panel depicted the departure of the horse and groom, but the executor of the next panel has also portrayed them. The posture of the dejected groom and the horse turning back to gaze at his master delicately convey feelings of poignant wistfulness.

Sakyamuni then cuts off his hair. (67) Next he discards his royal robes and puts on the orange robes of a passing hunter (in fact another god in disguise). (68) The prince's head in this relief has unfortunately been damaged. The nature scene on the right and the gods on the left are not required by the text.

The gods all come to applaud the prince. (69) Plants and animals frame the panel, in addition to two pots in a square frame which have no relationship to anything in known texts. The prince has now acquired his characteristic curly hairstyle; the bump on the head symbolizes his extraordinary wisdom.

The prince goes to two places where brahman female hermits offer him food to eat. (70) The Borobudur artists envisioned the hermitage in a wild mountain forest, as indicated by the trees, rock motifs, and wild animals on

the right side of the panel.

The prince embarks on a life as a wandering monk. Eventually he comes to a kingdom called Vaisali where he asks permission to become a pupil of a brahman named Arada Kalapa. (71) The mountainous jungle behind the prince suggests he has just emerged from there. The standing, bearded figure probably represents the brahman with disciples behind him. One of the latter holds out a water pitcher, of a type called *kendi,* to the prince. Until very recently it was common to see such pitchers placed near the roads in Java so that thirsty passers-by might take a drink.

After some time Arada acknowledges the prince as his equal and Sakyamuni becomes a teacher too. (72) In the relief the prince holds his hands in *abhaya mudra,* "dispelling fear," comforting the five pupils who are shown seated in caves. Arada sits on a stone throne of a type found in archaeological sites in recent Javanese palaces, usually called a *watu gilang,* a "shining stone."

Sakyamuni eventually decides to resume his travels. He comes to the city of Rajagrha to beg, and all the people are struck by his appearance. One man declares that Brahma himself has come to beg. The king comes to give alms to the prince. (73) The relief shows the palace on the far left, courtiers and citizens sitting about, then the queen and king, who holds a bowl of food.

The next day the king and many others see a bright light shining from Mount Pandava where Sakyamuni is staying. They go to him and invite him to stay and take

half the kingdom. (74) The relief shows the rocky scenery of the mountains, with various wild animals and the prince sitting in a cave. The king is in a supplicating posture on his left.

Sakyamuni next visits Rudraka, a teacher in Rajagrha, who invites Sakyamuni to join him. (75) Again the sculptor places the scene in a mountain forest rather than a city. Hermits, identifiable by their hair styles and beads, listen to his discourse.

Episode 4: Buddha's Enlightenment. *Panels 76-105, on the northern side of the monument.*

After some time the prince decides to go to Magadha. Five men from Rudraka's group decide to follow him, considering him the wiser teacher. The prince and his new disciples meditate on Gayasirsa Mountain. (76) In the relief, Sakyamuni and his five disciples are shown meditating in caves, with a flowing stream full of fish on the far right. These details were probably added by the Borobudur artists themselves, for they are not given in any existing versions of the story.

Then the six men go to meditate beside the Nairanjana River. Here Sakymuni practices such austerities that he nearly starves himself. (77) Sakyamuni's gesture indicates his steadfast refusal to cease his fast despite the pleas of his disciples.

Seeing that Sakyamuni is near death, the spirit of his mother, Queen Maya, now a goddess, comes to see him and begins to cry. The prince, however, reassures her that he will not die. (78) The episode of Buddha's near-death from starvation is frequently depicted by showing him in an emaciated form, sometimes rather gruesomely skeletal. Borobudur's sculptor portrayed his body as normal, which is consistent with the general avoidance of disturbing themes on Borobudur's reliefs. Queen Maya is accompanied by a large number of nymph attendants carrying various objects such as incense burners, fans, trays, flowers, fly whisks, etc.

Many other gods and supernatural beings also come to stay beside him. (79) The relief depicts only the gods, to whom the prince is lecturing.

The gods offer to provide the prince with magical strength so that he will not have to eat, but the prince declines out of fear that people living nearby will be misled into thinking that he can live without food. The prince then decides to cease his extreme asceticism. In disappointment, the five disciples leave him. (80)

Having abandoned his fast, the prince goes to a place called Uruvila, where the daughters of the village head

Left: *Borobudur's carvers often added embellishments that have no connection with the story being depicted, such as this charming group of animals.* (panel 83)

Opposite: *The bodhisattva on his horse as he makes his midnight escape from the palace.* (panel 65)

Sakyamuni practiced such severe asceticism that he was in danger of starving. First the spirit of his mother came to ask him to stop, but he refused. Next many gods and supernatural beings came to stay with him and offered to provide him with magical strength so that he would not have to eat, but he refused. Seated on the far left, Sakyamuni is shown making a gesture of refusal to the assembled deities who occupy the rest of the panel. (panel 79)

provide him with food. (81)

Sakyamuni decides to put on a new robe and chooses the shroud of a dead woman by the name of Radha, who had been a slave of a certain Sujata, the daughter of one of the village heads. He goes to a pond to wash it on a stone. When Sakyamuni tries to come out of the pond, however, the demon Mara makes the banks rise enormously high. He is saved by the goddess of a tree beside the pond, who bends her branch so that Sakyamuni can use it to climb out of the pond. (82)

Another god gives the prince a reddish robe, which he accepts. (83) The peacocks, monkeys and elephants on the far left are the artist's own elaborations.

Sujata, the village chief's daughter, dreams that Sakyamuni has ended his fasting. She sends a slave to invite the prince to her house, where she feeds him. (84) On the ground beside the prince is a dish with a highly decorated cover from which steam rises. The chieftain's house is elaborately decked with flags, and cooking is depicted in detail on the far right.

Sakyamuni returns to the Nairanjana River to bathe, taking with him a golden bowl which Sujata had given him although he did not want it. (85) The four kneeling figures are not required by the extant texts.

As he bathes, gods come to attend him. (86) As some gods sprinkle Sakyamuni with perfume and flowers,

other gods collect the water to make a relic of it. On the right bank, two *naga* "water spirits" raise their heads from the river, each depicted in conventional fashion with a jewel on their crowns.

Upon emerging from the river the prince seeks a place to sit, and the female *nagi* of the river gives him a bejeweled throne. (87) The large cushions on this and other thrones are depicted consistently in the reliefs, suggesting that such cushions must have been found in ancient Javanese palaces.

The prince sits down and finishes the food Sujata had given him. (88) The seat and the surroundings are represented quite differently from those in the previous relief,

despite the fact that it is the same place. Again, a small lion pops from a round den in the lower right.

When he is finished eating, Sakyamuni throws the golden bowl into the river. Sagara, the king of the *nagas* saves it, but Indra also desire it. First Indra turns himself into a *garuda* and tries to take it with the *vajra* "thunderbolt" in his beak. When he asks for it courteously, however, Sagara gives it to him to be placed in a reliquary. (89) On the right of the relief, Sakyamuni has just thrown the bowl into the river, where the *naga* king is picking it up. On the left he is presenting it to Indra, next to whom sits Airavata.

The prince then set off for the *bodhi* "enlightenment"

Following pages (left side): *The prince stands on a lotus cushion, cutting off his hair with a sword and discarding his royal clothing and crown. Gods swoop down to collect it on trays. On the right, the groom sits before the horse, holding the discarded crown and the sheath to the sword. (panel 67)*

Following pages (right side): *Sakyamuni bathes in the Nairanjana River, attended by gods who sprinkle him with perfume and flowers. On the right bank, two naga water spirits raise their heads from the river, each depicted with a jewel on their crowns. (panel 86)*

tree, and gods prepare the way for him. The prince wishes to take some grass to sit on. When he comes to a grass cutter named Svastika, he asks her for a bunch. (90)

In the extant texts this episode and the following one are given in reverse order from that in which they appear on the monument. Much of this relief is occupied by figures of gods not specifically mentioned as being present. The rock motifs on either side of the lotus cushion on which the prince stands probably indicate the path prepared by the gods.

Brahma and a group of gods go to pay homage to the prince. The *naga* king Kalika, seeing the prince radiating with light, goes to pay his respects too. He is surrounded by a multitude of gods including Brahma and Indra. (91) The god kneeling in front of Sakyamuni is Brahma, clearly recognizable from his hairdo. The four figures at the far left are the *naga* king and three of his followers, again marked by their headdresses. The curious object the *naga* king holds in his hands is obviously a mark of honor, but we do not know exactly what it symbolized or whether any such objects existed in ancient Java. The three discus-like top pieces for some of the staffs are known from bronze examples.

Now it is time for Sakyamuni to seek a tree under which to meditate. Many gods each decorate a *bodhi* tree in the hope that Sakyamuni will sit under his. (92)

To avoid causing disappointment to any of the gods, Sakyamuni makes his image appear to sit under each tree. As he meditates, bodhisattvas come to pay their respects to him. (93)

The demon Mara attacks the prince in a final effort to prevent Sakyamuni from achieving enlightenment. Sakyamuni remonstrates with the demon, recalling that Mara had been made ruler of the Kingdom of Desire in return for a single sacrifice in a former life, but that he himself had made millions of sacrifices in his former lives. Mara replies that Sakyamuni himself was a witness to Mara's sacrifice, but that no one there could serve as witness for Sakyamuni, so Sakyamuni must submit. Sakyamuni responds by touching the earth with his right hand. The earth goddess Sthavara appears with many other goddesses, each of whom testify to his innumerable sacrifices for others. (94)

Having failed to defeat Sakyamuni by force, Mara sends his beautiful daughters to try to arouse him to passion, but this too fails. (95)

Sakyamuni then attains Supreme Enlightenment and becomes Buddha, the "Enlightened One." (96) Other buddhas send many umbrellas ornamented with gems to shelter the scene of his enlightenment. (97) These are depicted floating in the air above the many nymphs who come to pay homage. The lotus cushions and blossoms in the air are not mentioned in extant texts.

The gods bathe Buddha with perfumed water. (98) One of the gods asks Buddha what meditation he had used to remain in the same position for seven days. Buddha responds with its name: *prityaharavyuha*. (99) In the relief Buddha changes his hand to a *mudra* betokening "dispelling fear."

Soon Buddha arises to walk, twice covering miraculous distances, but both times returning to the sacred Bodhimanda. (100)

Four weeks after attaining enlightenment, Buddha goes to stay with a *naga* king named Mucilinda. The weather being poor, the *naga* king winds himself around Buddha to protect him as he meditates. (101) This scene is often depicted in three-dimensional sculptures with Buddha seated on the coils of a seven-headed cobra. On Borobudur a different design is employed: the *naga* king

is portrayed bowing before Buddha who sits in a pavilion. The elephant and writhing dwarf in the scene have not been satisfactorily explained.

Five weeks after his enlightenment, Buddha leaves Mucilinda's palace to walk to a banyan tree. On the way he meets ascetics who ask him how he has borne the week of bad weather. (102)

Buddha goes to meditate under another tree. A caravan of merchants passes by, and they are frightened by various portents, but a goddess reassures them. (103) Rays of light stream out from the tree, reflecting Buddha's brilliance. The merchants are the three men on the far right of the panel shown talking to a woman representing the goddess.

The merchants offer Buddha food. He wants a stone bowl to put it in and four gods—the "Great Kings" or "Guardians of the Four Directions"—each offer such bowls. Not wanting to offend any of them, he takes the four and combines them into one. (104) The merchants give honey and cream to Buddha. (105)

Episode 5: The Preaching of the First Sermon. *Panels 106-120, on the eastern side of the monument to the north of the stairway.*

That night the gods, led by Brahma and Indra, ask Buddha to preach the Law. (106) None of the gods are specifically identified in this relief. Buddha is now in *dhyani mudra*, signifying meditation.

At first he does not reply, but near morning he agrees to preach. (107) Again no specific gods are identifiable.

Buddha then asks to whom he should first preach the Law. Rudraka, his first choice, has been dead for a week. Next he asks for Arada Kalapa, but he too has been dead for three days. Then he asks for his five earlier disciples, and by using his supernatural vision he sees that they are in the Deer Park at Benares. (108) This may be the intent of this relief, but there is no specific evidence for this interpretation.

Buddha sets off for Benares. (109) On the way he meets a monk who asks where he is going. (110) Later he passes through Gaya and is hosted by a *naga* king named Sudarsana. (111) Rows of *nagas* are shown bringing gifts.

Buddha goes through several other cities and is honored in each of them. (112-114) The events in these cities are not specifically described in the extant text, but the Borobudur designers devoted three relief panels to such celebrations. Perhaps they were more fully discussed in the Javanese version of the text. Panel 112 shows a huge feast set out under umbrellas beneath a pavilion roof. The

temple-like building on the far left may indicate that the scene is taking place in a city.

When Buddha comes to the River Ganges, the ferryman refuses to row him across without payment. Buddha simply flies across the river and the boatman faints out of shame. (115)

Buddha arrives at Benares and goes to beg for food. (116) Then he finds his five former disciples, who caustically remark: "Here comes the worthy monk Gautama, the lazy one, the glutton, spoiled by his indolence. Let no one go to meet him or rise when he comes or relieve him of his bowl…." (117) As shown in the relief, they are not taking any special trouble to greet him.

When Buddha comes near they are all awed by his radiance and cannot restrain themselves from arising and serving him. Their long hair, characteristic of forest-dwelling ascetics, is magically shorn and monks' robes appear on them. (118) The relief shows how the disciples have been transformed in appearance. Buddha is speaking to them, as shown by his *vitarka mudra*.

The disciples ceremonially bathe Buddha. (119) This scene is depicted on Borobudur as taking place in a lotus pond. The four water spirits (*nagas*) shown are not cited in extant texts.

Then Buddha preaches the first sermon, which sets the "Wheel of the Law" in motion. (120) The disciples are depicted in the lower left corner listening to the sermon. Unfortunately this relief has been badly damaged, especially the central figure of Buddha.

Here the narrative ends, at the corner of the east staircase. Some analysts have expressed surprise that the story ends here in what they consider an abrupt fashion. Important events from Buddha's later life, such as his entry into Nirvana, are omitted.

Nirvana is a goal more emphasized in the "Elder Doctrine" than in Mahayana Buddhism, however. Mahayana philosophy is concerned with selfless bodhisattvas who refuse to enter Nirvana in order to save other beings. Buddha's greatest deed according to Mahayana Buddhism was to preach the "Law of Salvation." His later entry into Nirvana was almost an act of self-indulgence by comparison.

Opposite: *A detail showing the citizens of Benares paying homage to Buddha.* (panel 116)

Above: *Gautama comes upon his five former disciples, who left him after he renounced his asceticism. They are all depicted with long hair as forest-dwelling ascetics. At first they resolve to show him no respect, but quickly find themselves drawn to follow him again. In the relief the disciples' expressions seem to be caught at the very moment of transformation from studied indifference to wonder and awe.* (panel 117)

The Gandavyuha
Travels of a Young Man in Search of Wisdom

OF ALL THE STORIES TOLD ON BOROBUDUR, the Javanese devoted the most space to a tale about a youth named Sudhana and his quest for wisdom. They reserved the three highest galleries for it, obviously feeling the greatest respect for this story about a boy who travels far and visits many teachers in search of knowledge.

The sculptors were given 460 panels in which to tell Sudhana's story. It begins on the main wall of the second gallery (128 panels), continues on the main wall (88 panels) and balustrade (88 panels) of the third gallery, fills the balustrade of the fourth gallery (84 panels), and then reaches its conclusion on the main wall of the fourth gallery (72 panels).

The literary work which the artists illustrated is entitled the *Gandavyuha*, "The Structure of the World Compared to a Bubble." The narrative interest of the story does not compare with that of stories told in the lower galleries of Borobudur. There are no adventures or romances, just repetitive visits to various teachers, alternating with mystical visions experienced by Sudhana and others. Moreover, the text describes these in abstract language quite unsuited for providing sculptors with sharp images to engrave in stone.

One can imagine that pilgrims who had absorbed the morals contained in the fairytales and in the story of Prince Gautama in the lower galleries were now thought to be ready for more solemn and technical intellectual fare. Having been entertained, they were expected to apply themselves to more rigorous studies. The lower reliefs may have been intended to provide an introduction in easily understandable form to concepts and terminology which would now be explained in didactic fashion.

The *Gandavyuha* begins with Buddha and Samantabhadra ("Universally Good") in a garden with Manjusri and virtuous human kings, surrounded by 5,000 bodhisattvas. They ask Buddha to perform a miracle for them, which he does by going into a meditation called "the appearance of the lion," causing beautiful visions to appear. Most of the scripture is a repetitive account of Sudhana's long journey to visit many spiritual instructors, called *kalyanamitra* ("Good Friends") in the text, each of whom imparts wisdom to him before sending him on to the next guru. Sudhana eventually reaches the heavenly palace of Maitreya, the next Buddha.

One of the most interesting features of Borobudur is the difference in emphasis which the Javanese have placed on certain parts of this story compared to the written versions that have come down to us. Extant versions of the text focus almost all their attention on Sudhana's visits to his teachers before he reaches Maitreya's palace. Only about one-tenth of the narrative describes what happens once Sudhana gets there.

The emphasis in the Borobudur reliefs is quite the opposite. Sudhana's pilgrimages are allotted only 126 of the panels, while the remaining 334 panels depict scenes and events which take place after Sudhana's arrival at Maitreya's palace, as well as his meetings with two other supernatural teachers: the buddha Manjusri and the bodhisattva Samantabhadra. It is Samantabhadra who has the honor of imparting the highest wisdom to Sudhana. The climax of the entire series of 1,460 reliefs on Borobudur comes when Sudhana vows to follow the example of Samantabhadra.

Opposite: *Royal attendants, distinctive for their unusual hairstyle (high coil on top, short fringe in front), carrying various objects. One carries a shield, another a covered bowl. All look raptly toward the main action of the scene. Many of Borobudur's pilgrims would have identified themselves with onlookers such as these found in most reliefs.*

Preceding pages: *A scene from one of Maitreya's past lives, as a ruler in a palace. Mythical half-human birds (kinnaras) fly above the pavilion. Dancers and musicians are depicted in a scene that was undoubtedly familiar to Borobudur's artists. (panel III.65)*

Sudhana visits a number of Night Goddesses, who appear in dreams to announce that someone has just attained enlightenment. Sudhana, on the left of the panel, assumes his characteristic position when visiting "Good Friends": kneeling with both hands on the floor. The goddess sits in a pavilion on a lion throne. Her left hand is raised in a gesture indicating that she is teaching Sudhana. The curling motifs at the top corners represent clouds. (panel II.67)

The Text The *Gandavyuha* was one of the most widely distributed Buddhist scriptures in all Asia. Scenes from it are illustrated in many ancient Chinese and Japanese works of art, but are depicted quite differently on Borobudur. Sometimes the *Gandavyuha* was a separate work, but more often it formed the conclusion of an important text called the *Avatamsaka Sutra*, the "Flower Ornament Scripture." The oldest preserved versions of the text are Chinese translations from Sanskrit originals.

The *Gandavyuha* was first translated into Chinese as a separate work in the fourth century. The first complete translation of the *Avatamsaka Sutra* was finished in A.D. 421 by Buddhabhadra, a north Indian monk. The *Gandavyuha* forms the last of the text's 34 chapters.

A further complication results from the fact that the last part of the version of the *Gandavyuha* illustrated on Borobudur is not found in the *Avatamsaka Sutra*, nor even in two of the three oldest Chinese translations of the *Gandavyuha*. This last section is the *Bhadracari Pranidhanagatha* ("Samantabhadra's Vow"), often shortened to *Bhadracari*. Even more confusingly, the last part of the *Bhadracari*, which concerns the power and glory of Buddha Amitabha, is left out of the early versions and first appeared separately in a translation produced by Amoghavajra in the eighth century. A complete version of the *Gandavyuha* was only translated into Chinese in A.D. 798 by a monk named Prajna, who worked from a manuscript given to the Chinese emperor by the king of

Orissa. This is of course contemporary with the construction of Borobudur, indicating that the Javanese probably had a complete version before the Chinese did.[3]

The Story of Sudhana

In the first series of 16 panels, running from the east stairway to the southeast corner, a group of celestial beings are shown in a forest with Buddha as he meditates, performs miracles for them, and is worshipped by crowds of bodhisattvas, disciples, and virtuous human rulers. Some of the humans who are followers of the Elder Doctrine cannot see the miracles, however. The scripture says they were unable to see the miracles because they only sought salvation for themselves and did not think of helping others. Their minds were also not prepared for seeing visions beyond their own previous experiences. This may be the point of the second relief panel (II.2), in which Buddha has become invisible. Only his empty throne remains. Visitors to the monument were probably told that this meant they should now prepare themselves mentally for new insights. They should be ready to give up their former mental habits and ways of seeing the world to make way for new experiences which the following reliefs would show them.

In the last relief, before one rounds the southeast corner, an important bodhisattva named Manjusri is shown sitting in his tower. He decides to go to the human realm to the south. The names of places mentioned later in the scripture are indeed located in South India. He stays at a shrine east of the city where many people come to worship him, including the boy Sudhana, whose name means "Good Wealth." As Manjusri says, when Sudhana was born many jewels appeared magically in his parents' house. Just as Manjusri is about to leave, Sudhana speaks, asking him for guidance to perfect himself and obtain the "thunderbolt of knowledge" which he believes can shatter the preconceptions which burden people and keep them ignorant. Manjusri tells Sudhana to visit a monk who lives on a mountain in a nearby country.

In this panel, Sudhana is shown standing on the right along with a group of attendants. They are never mentioned in the text, however, and do not appear in illustrations from China or Japan. (II.16)

The panels on the south face of the monument illustrate Sudhana's visits to the first Good Friends to whom Manjusri sends him for instruction. The scripture never mentions his means of transportation, but on Borobudur Sudhana is depicted traveling by various means: walking, in a sedan chair, on an elephant, and in a carriage. These

scenes are probably Javanese additions.

The sequence of visits to 45 Good Friends only occurs once in the texts, but it is repeated a second time on Borobudur. This may have been done in order to make the number of panels between Sudhana's first visit to a Good Friend and his arrival at Maitreya's celestial palace equal 110. One passage in the text mentions that he visited 110 Good Friends, but only 45 are actually described. Thus to make the number of visits equal the ideal total, the sculptors made Sudhana repeat the entire pilgrimage.

A lesson which the scripture implies is that one should not expect to find enlightenment only in one place, or from one source. Sudhana's Good Friends are women, men and children from all levels of society, as well as supernatural beings. Anyone is eligible for enlightenment and there is no suggestion that wisdom is something to be jealously hoarded and imparted only to the elite.

The scripture frequently makes the point, however, that different people have varying capacities for understanding Buddhist teachings, and that the lessons have to be adapted to the level of the student. Thus Borobudur does not seem to have been meant only for learned religious students, but was also for those visitors who reached this level of the monument. They would have needed to have an open mind in order to benefit from the instructions of the reliefs on the upper galleries.

In the first stage of his quest, Sudhana's teachers are

The bodhisattva Manjusri appears, sitting in his tower, and instructs Sudhana to visit a monk who lives on a mountain. In this panel, Manjusri is portrayed in a very distinctive way, his face and body quite unlike any other man depicted on Borobudur. One has the feeling that he may have been modelled after a living person, perhaps an important dignitary of the Sailendra kingdom which built Borobudur. He wears a yogapattra *cord around his knee and sits on a lotus flower on a throne decorated with* makaras *on the backrest and jewel motifs on the base. The throne is inside a pavilion which has more* makaras. *His left hand holds the stem of a blue lotus—identified by its shape—while his right hand is flexed in a gesture which has no particular symbolism. Monks sit beneath a tree to the left while Sudhana stands on the right, his face unfortunately obliterated. (panel II.16)*

An unidentified scene, probably depicting one of Sudhana's visits to a Good Friend—a royal personage on an ornate throne. (panel II.87)

human: monks (II.17-19,22), doctors (II.20), *rsi* (II.24), laity (II.29), nuns (II.33), kings (II.35-36), hermits (II.39), and a princess—but also common people, such as merchants like his father, a ship's captain (II.41), and even a young boy (II.27). Sudhana also worships a stupa. (II.45)

Sudhana's journey continually takes him further southward until he confronts two divine beings. His meetings with them are shown at the far corner of the south face. One is the bodhisattva Avalokitesvara (II.47), who lives on the Potalaka Mountain. The other is Siva, the most popular Hindu god in Java (II.48), whom he

finds preaching in a city temple.

The first scenes encountered when the visitor turns the corner show Sudhana's visits to various goddesses. There are not enough clues in the depictions for us to be certain of the identity of the Good Friend in each relief, but some of the possibilities include the Earth Goddess (II.49), Gautama Buddha's wife (II.62), his mother (II.63), and eight Goddesses of the Night (II.50-57). The Goddesses of the Night appear in dreams and awaken people to announce that a particular person had just achieved enlightenment. (II.67) Sudhana finds all of them in

Magadha. Two sit in a mandala surrounding Vairocana, two in a mandala around Buddha, who the scripture says is Vairocana's manifestation in human form. At one point Sudhana ascends to the "Heaven of the 33 Kings" to see a goddess, then returns to earth at Kapilavastu. He then resumes a southward route, visiting more Good Friends, including a goldsmith and simple villagers. His final visit is to a boy and girl who send him to Maitreya.

Then follows a series of reliefs in which Sudhana is absent, probably indicating a transition to a different section of the text. These scenes depict people walking on clouds (II.73), a buddha flanked by four bodhisattvas sitting on lotuses (II.74), teaching (II.75), and being worshipped (II.76). Sudhana reappears, and then begins a second sequence of visits to Good Friends, including hermits, merchants, Avalokitesvara (II.100-102) and Siva (II.104). There are also scenes of Sudhana worshipping Buddha (II.78, 94) and a stupa (II.96, 98).

On the east gallery Sudhana visits more goddesses and a number of people who cannot be identified. In one episode, a Goddess of the Night is portrayed sitting in a building decorated with *vajras*. (II.106) In another, a bod-

A detail showing Sudhana's attendants, who are not mentioned in extant versions of the Gandavyuha *text. On Borobudur, however, Sudhana is never without them.*

hisattva named Vimaladhvaja is shown attaining enlightenment. (II.113) In the last three reliefs before the gateway (II.126-128), Sudhana comes to Vairocana's Jewel Tower to see Maitreya, who will be his mentor on the next series of reliefs on level three.

The *Gandhavyuha* continues on the main wall of the third gallery. All the panels of this level on both sides of the walkway are allocated to just one theme: Sudhana's visit to Maitreya. In the reliefs on the east face south of the stairway, Sudhana pays homage to Maitreya (III.1), listens to a lecture (III.2), and is told that he may now enter the tower. (III.3)

Maitreya opens the gates by snapping his fingers (III.4), an old custom in India where people used to snap their fingers before entering a room to avoid startling those who might be within. The symbolism of snapping one's fingers has deeper implications. According to some scriptures Buddha attained enlightenment when deities snapped their fingers. Here it symbolizes both the opening of the door and the enlightening experiences Sudhana will have inside the Jewel Tower.

Maitreya tells Sudhana that the door is now open (III.5) and he happily climbs up the steps. (III.6) Sudhana looks around the inside of the tower, which contains many other palaces. (III.7) Maitreya gives Sudhana another lesson (III.8-9). A number of panels then follow (III.8-19), the meanings of which are not entirely clear. They may portray Maitreya's instructions to Sudhana for further travels.

Upon turning the corner, one sees more panels depicting Maitreya instructing Sudhana. Sudhana will first visit the Buddha Manjusri (foreshadowed in III.12). He will ultimately become the protégé of another bodhisattva, Samantabhadra. (III.16-19) Samantabhadra is given a particularly important place on Borobudur, since he appears on the highest level of the entire series of narrative reliefs. He is identifiable by the long-stemmed flower with three blossoms which he holds in his left hand.

Now begins a long series of reliefs devoted to illustrating lists of things. The first 20 panels portray various decorations in Vairocana's Jewel Tower. On the south side these include flags, bells (III.22), garlands of pearls (III.23-24), jewels, nets of gold (III.24?), incense burners (III.25), mirrors (III.27), altars, clouds of precious cloth (III.29), jewel trees (III.30) and banners (III.31).

The enumeration of objects in the Jewel Tower continues on the west face and includes golden banana trees (III.33), statues of bodhisattvas made of jewels (III.34), songbirds (III.35), jewel lotuses (III.36), and lotus ponds

Opposite: *Avalokitesvara, one of the most popular Buddhist deities in Asia. He was a bodhisattva who lived on Mount Potalaka, and was known for his compassion. Here he is shown seated on a lion throne in a six-armed form. His lower-right hand is in the position representing charity, his upper right hand holds a rosary, and his middle left hand holds the stem of a lotus—the blossom of which is beside his head. Celestial beings soar above. (panel II.102)*

Following page: *The bodhisattva Vimaladhvaja in meditation, while two armies battle fiercely. (panel II.113)*

(III.38). Next follows a series of reliefs in which Sudhana sees the spiritual advances Maitreya made in his past lives by meditating, being charitable (III.44), worshipping Buddha (III.45), and practicing yoga. (III.47) Many of the reliefs of this section are difficult to identify precisely.

In one tower Maitreya appears as a universal monarch guiding his people (III.59); in others he appears in different forms as he preaches to titans, the perennial adversaries of the gods. (III.68) He eases the suffering of beings tortured in the underworld (III.69) and gives food to the hungry ghosts. (III.70) He preaches to various categories of creatures including animals (III.71), humans (III.72), *nagas* (III.74), and a group of gods, ogres, birds, titans, and humans. (III.75)

The rest of the panels on the main wall of the third gallery (east face, north of the stairway) are not easy to interpret. They show Maitreya teaching more groups of beings who approach enlightenment. The last three reliefs (III.86-88) may show Maitreya with a group of bodhisattvas discussing artistic and scientific ways to benefit all beings; Maitreya with a group of bodhisattvas who will be enlightened in one lifetime; and Maitreya walking without stopping for thousands of centuries.

The sequence continues on the balustrade of the third gallery, again beginning at the east staircase and proceeding south. The reliefs are badly damaged. Some are completely missing while others are fragmentary. Some might even be out of sequence. When van Erp restored this section between 1907-1911, he had no guidance since the source of these reliefs had not yet been identified. It is surprising that he achieved such accurate results considering the circumstances under which he had to work.

The first panel on the east side begins with two figures, perhaps Sudhana kneeling and Maitreya standing. The reliefs are difficult to interpret, since the scripture illustrated here is highly abstract. It mentions Sudhana's visions of bodhisattvas from whose bodies countless supernatural beings and humans appear, along with the sound of teaching the doctrine.

In one tower Sudhana sees a vision of Maitreya being born in a lotus (IIIB.35?), and taking seven steps in an echo of Gautama's first act. This might be depicted in IIIB.34; if so, the reconstruction has reversed them. The two men standing to the left might be the gods Indra and Brahma, who are said to have watched him walk.

The next reliefs illustrate a sequence of visions in which Sudhana sees figures of Buddha (IIIB.47, 50), bodhisattvas, other supernatural beings, and all sorts of humans seated on lotuses. He also sees Jewel Trees with

Above: *Maitreya in a previous incarnation, performing the difficult physical yoga of a future bodhisattva, in this case standing upon one foot. (panel III.47)*

Opposite: *A past incarnation of Maitreya as an earthly king. (panel III.65)*

Preceding page: *Dancers in Maitreya's palace. (panel III.65)*

various beings in their crowns (IIIB.64,66-67; 51 may also belong here).

The series continues on the east balustrade. This illustrates things which Maitreya gave to those in need in his past lives, beginning with his own head. (IIIB.71) The next panels cannot be precisely interpreted, but should show gifts of clothing, jewelry, etc. In IIIB.80 he has given parts of himself to ogres to eat; in IIIB.84 he is giving away his child, in IIIB.85 his wife, in IIIB.86 piles of jewels and in IIIB.88 his palace (or perhaps his entire kingdom).

The text continues on the balustrade of the fourth level. The first reliefs from the staircase to the southeastern corner illustrate more of Maitreya's gifts. The first gift, to a brahman, is "Universal Monarchy"—symbolized by a palace and the seven emblems of a ruler, which

are a queen, army commander, chief minister, elephant, discus, horse, and a wish-granting jewel. (IVB.1) Then he gives his throne to a monk. (IVB.2) The next reliefs may represent servants, his palace and concubines, and his gardens. (IVB.3-4) In IVB.5 he gives parasols. Other gifts include flowers, perfume, medicine and food (IVB.9-11), shelter (IVB.14), valuable copper containers (IVB.16), and a conveyance (depicted as a carriage. (IVB.17)

The panels on the south side of the fourth balustrade portray another sequence of virtuous deeds performed by Maitreya. These include setting prisoners free (IVB.18), treating sick children (IVB.19), and showing lost travellers the correct path. (IVB.20)

According to the text, the next panel should show Maitreya as a boatman ferrying people across the river, but here he seems to be carrying them physically.

Above: *Bodhisattvas preach the scripture to all forms of beings. Here Sudhana observes as Maitreya (not shown) preaches, while wild animals listen raptly. (panel III.71)*

Opposite: *Maitreya demonstrating another act performed by all bodhisattvas: walking for millennia without stopping. Sudhana kneels and pays respect. (panel III.88)*

(IVB.21) The following panel depicts Maitreya as a horse, rescuing people from an island of demons. (IVB.22)

The pilgrim who persevered to the west balustrade of this level saw Maitreya as a wise teacher (IVB. 24), in the form of a buddha, (IVB.28-29), decorating monuments (here a stupa, IVB.33), and having statues of Buddha made. (IVB.34) The next few reliefs are difficult to interpret. The scripture mentions Maitreya teaching, and compares Sudhana's feelings to a person in a dream who sees certain things. One of these is a fine house (perhaps represented by IVB.36 or 38); another mentions music and dancing. (IVB.42)

Then Maitreya reappears and breaks Sudhana's spell

Above: *Samantabhadra's vow. He sits in the bottom center with his three-stemmed flower. Sudhana is on his left. Above him are nine buddhas in two rows. Those in back are all in* dharmacakra mudra; *those in front are in* mudras *corresponding to the four* jina *buddhas on Borobudur's four lower walls, plus the fifth on the upper wall. No one has succeeded in determining which part of the text this relief depicts. (panel IV.53)*

by snapping his fingers again. Maitreya instructs Sudhana to see Manjusri once more. The figure in the center of the next three panels (IVB.43-45) probably represents Manjusri with his boy's cords across his chest. Sudhana bids farewell to Maitreya. (IVB. 47)

On his way to see Manjusri, Sudhana passes through more than 110 cities. While he is still 110 leagues away (IVB.50), Manjusri stretches out his hand to touch Sudhana's head (IVB.51). They talk, but their conversation is only very briefly summarized in the text.

Now begins the final part of the scripture. Sudhana sits, contemplating the place where Buddha attained enlightenment and wishing to see the bodhisattva Samantabhadra. As he meditates (IVB.52-53), Sudhana begins to have visions preparing him for Samantabhadra's appearance. These are ten visions of Buddha lands, some of which have lotus ponds. (IVB.54)

These visions continue around the corner on the north

side, where we see a site of enlightenment (IVB.61) and other representations of more abstract concepts, such as kind people. One vision shows beings absorbed in contemplating Buddha. (IVB.62) Next Sudhana sees ten bright lights, some in the form of flowers and jewels (IVB.63), and others that are more difficult to depict, such as perfumes.

Just on the east side of the north gate Sudhana finally sees Samantabhadra (IVB.70 or 71) sitting in front of

Vairocana. (IVB.72) Then follow yet more miraculous scenes: clouds of fragrant trees with incense burners (IVB.73), clothes, pearls, wish-granting jewels, and many other lands and celestial beings.

On the panels of the northeast balustrade, Sudhana finally attains the perfection of the ten stages of knowledge. (IVB.81) Then Samantabhadra touches Sudhana on the head. (IVB.82) The next two reliefs show buddhas in the four *mudras* symbolic of the four main directions.

Beginning at the east gate, the main wall of the fourth gallery illustrates the last part of the *Gandavyuha*. Sudhana has become one with Samantabhadra, who pronounces a vow. It begins with an expression of homage to the buddhas of the ten directions (perhaps illustrated by the ten buddhas in IV.1). Then he refers to buddhas sitting among bodhisattvas (IV.2,3) and promises offerings—flowers (IV.5), garlands (IV.6), music (IV.7), and parasols (IV.9)—to all buddhas.

Around the corner on the south face, the first relief depicts Samantabhadra seated to the right of a stupa. This may represent the offering of a basket of incense as large as a mountain which the text mentions. (IV.13) More buddhas and offerings appear. The text contains more pious wishes for the good of all creatures. Samantabhadra vows to teach serpent beings (IV.31), ogres (IV.32-33),

Above: *Detail from another panel showing Samantabhadra's vow. A buddha makes the* bhumisparsa mudra, *observed by a saintly royal figure at right. (panel IV.54)*

Following pages (left side): *One of a series of reliefs in which Maitreya shows Sudhana scenes from his past lives as examples of the good deeds a bodhisattva should perform. These include meditation, charity, worshipping Buddha, and practicing physical yoga. This particular relief may indicate the virtue of reading; a man standing under a parasol just behind Sudhana is holding objects which may be books. (panel III.49)*

Following pages (right side): *These last reliefs on Borobudur are very difficult to interpret. They represent highly abstract portions of the Gandavyuha which describe the appearance of uncountable buddhas from around the universe. They are shown with various symbols such as stupas, suns, and moons which are difficult to account for. (panel IV.72)*

One in a series of panels illustrating Sudhana and Samantabhadra's vows to do good deeds. Scholars have not succeeded in explaining many of these panels. This one may portray a wish to see the buddhas of the past, present, and future, represented by the three figures seated in the top half of the panel. Samantabhadra sits below in the center, identified by his three-stemmed flower. (panel IV.50)

humans (IV.34), and all other beings. (IV.35)

It is very difficult to correlate the reliefs on the west and north faces with specific parts of the text. Sudhana makes pious wishes to perform such acts as "traversing the paths of the world free from compulsion, affliction, and delusion, like a lotus unstained by water, like the sun and moon unattached in the sky," and to preserve the true teaching of the buddhas.

On the east face, the reliefs conclude with the final passage from the *Gandavyuha* in which Buddha himself tells Sudhana that all bodhisattvas, monks, and the great

disciples are elated and applaud the vow which he and Samantabhadra have made. (IV.72) No doubt pilgrims who reached this stage of instruction now identified themselves with Sudhana, and felt that by their perserverence, they too had given all the buddhas cause for joy.

We do not know what came next, but we can imagine that the pilgrims ascended to the round terraces at the top of the monument. There, their long journey at a successful end, their visit to Borobudur reached its climax, perhaps with the laying of offerings around the edge of the great central stupa.

Left: *Sudhana expresses the wish to acquire the power to fly like Samantabhadra. The relief depicts Samantabhadra demonstrating his ability to fly while Sudhana looks on respectfully. (panel IV.60)*

APPENDIX A
Survey of Javanese Art

Those visitors to Borobudur who will not have an opportunity to visit more than a few temples in central Java will be deprived of the chance of seeing the position Borobudur occupies in the broader world of early Javanese art and civilization.

Hardly any Javanese works of art can be dated. A mere handful of monuments and sculptures have dates inscribed on them. Most of the major sites of Borobudur's period were excavated in the early twentieth century before archaeologists began to apply scientific techniques in their explorations. Monuments and statues were unearthed without any proper records of their precise relationship to one another or to the different layers of soil. Without these details we cannot hope to reconstruct the history of Javanese art with any accuracy.

Thus we are forced to fall back upon less precise and reliable methods to estimate the dates of works of art. Buddhist and Hindu Javanese art is usually divided into two periods: the central Java period, between A.D. 700 and 900, and the east Java period, which lasted from 900 until 1500. Thereafter Javanese art entered the Islamic phase.

Most of the temples and sculptures of the central Javanese period are found in the interior of the island between the Dieng Plateau in the west and Mt. Lawu in the east, but there are a few examples several hundred kilometers further east. The extant examples of central Javanese art were mostly used for religious purposes. The principal exceptions are large numbers of gold jewelry: rings for fingers, toes, and ears, headdresses, necklaces, hair ornaments and cords for the waist and chest. All these, including a gold merchant's shop, can be seen on the reliefs of Borobudur.

There are other monuments with architectural forms like Borobudur's on the Asian mainland, but ironically there are no others in Indonesia. It seems that the Javanese were content with one such structure. The other buildings which remain from the central Javanese period are more conventional in that they contain rooms to house cult objects, perhaps to hide them from profane eyes.

Buddhist Temples The only two ancient temples left standing near Borobudur are Mendut and Pawon. Both were built around the same time as Borobudur, but each has a different shape. Pawon is small and has windows—an unusual feature found in few surviving Javanese temples—but no narrative reliefs. Mendut is very large and houses the three biggest Buddhist statues preserved intact on Java. Its stair walls are decorated with narrative reliefs from the *Birth Stories*.

In the Prambanan Plain, the best-preserved Buddhist temples are Kalasan, Sari, Sewu and Plaosan. All are decorated on the exterior with carvings of bodhisattvas, but have no narrative reliefs. Sari and Plaosan had provision for a second interior story with a wooden floor, but it has since disappeared. All originally consisted of one main sanctuary (or in Plaosan's case two) surrounded by many smaller temples and stupas, but at Kalasan and Sari the subsidiary buildings have disappeared.

Hindu Temples Except for the great Loro Jonggrang complex at Prambanan, the Hindu temples of central Java are smaller in size, but more numerous than the Buddhist temples. They span a longer period as well, from the late seventh to the late ninth century. Whereas the Buddhist temples are concentrated in the two broad plains in the middle of the island, near the probable centers of royal power, many of the Hindu temples are located in relatively remote areas and were probably built by local authorities. The Hindu architects formulated a standard plan at an early stage, which they followed later with minor variations in both small and great monuments. The central cult object was usually a *linggum*, a phallic symbol of Siva, although at Loro Jonggrang the main cult object was a statue of Siva. Around him were placed statues of the teacher Agastya on the south and Durga, the female essence of Siva, in the act of slaying the bull demon on the north. The entrance to the temple might be either on the east or west; opposite the entrance was an image of Ganesha, Siva's elephant-headed son, who helped men to overcome obstacles.

Among all the Hindu temples of central Java, only the Loro Jonggrang complex had a series of narrative reliefs. These begin on the main temple, where they depict the *Ramayana*—the story of Rama's attempt to regain his throne and his wife after he is wrongfully deprived of both. The story continues on the next temple, dedicated to the second member of the Hindu trinity, Brahma. On a third temple, dedicated to Vishnu, are reliefs depicting the life of Vishnu in his incarnation as Krishna.

The East Javanese Period No important temples of the early east Javanese period have been discovered. After central Javanese civilization vanished, several centuries passed before more monuments were built in east Java. By this time Javanese religion had undergone important changes. The gap between the elite and the commoners seems to have been much wider in east Java; many temples may have been meant mainly as places for the nobility to conduct secret rituals. The forms of architecture and sculpture had evolved far from those in central Java. Almost all the east Javanese temples were built of brick instead of the basaltic stone which the central Javanese chose as their principal building material.

There are no symmetrical complexes in east Java like Loro Jonggrang or Sewu, but there are large irregular temple groups such as the one at Panataran, near Blitar. Many of these temples were built as memorials dedicated to specific deceased rulers. There is no evidence that such beliefs had been prominent in central Java.

One of the few stone temples built in east Java was erected at Singhasari, near Malang, in memory of the assassinated last ruler of that kingdom; his body was never found. Others of brick are scattered over the valleys of the Brantas and Solo Rivers.

The greatest kingdom to appear in pre-Islamic Indonesia was named Majapahit. During the 14th century Majapahit claimed suzerainty over an area larger than modern Indonesia. Two types of temples were built in Majapahit. One type is found at such lowland sites as Trowulan (the capital), Jago, Kidal and Jawi. The forms of these temples are generally similar to the Hindu temples of central Java. The other type of temple was built on the upper slopes of mountains, where esoteric forms of worship took place. Examples include Sukuh and Cetoh on Mt. Lawu, and numerous complexes on such east Javanese mountains as Penanggungan, Ringgit, Arjuna and Argapura. These simpler sanctuaries were wooden pavilions. Their major structures were simply stone terraces, with three to seven levels ascending the mountainside toward the peak, with one to three altars on the topmost terrace. We can still detect a faint echo of Borobudur in this terraced form, even though the rituals performed at these sites would have seemed completely foreign to an Indian.

In spite of the fact that the statuary at these sites shows no trace of the grace and serenity of the central Javanese examples, the terraced form of these monuments may indicate that a faint memory of Borobudur persisted. Meanwhile, trees and volcanic ash were gradually drawing their shroud over the site and Borobudur was sleeping the long sleep which would only end when Cornelius arrived in 1814.

APPENDIX B
The World of Mandalas

The Matrix World or Dharma Dhatu Mandala
According to the *Mahavairocana* scripture, the diagram drawn on the ground with colored powder was to be divided into 81 squares, organized in concentric groups—nine in the center, then outer rings of 16, 24 and 32. On the first day, the master of the ceremony performed a ritual to awaken the gods who occupied the space where the diagram was to be set up, in order to obtain their assistance. On the third day he dug a small hole in the ground into which he put five precious materials, five fragrant things,[1] five medicines, and five grains, all in small containers of porcelain, gold or silver. The hole was then filled, and on top of it an initiation vase was placed with five more gems, perfumes, medicines, and grains. Sandalwood powder was used to mark critical locations—the places where images of buddhas and bodhisattvas should be put.

On the fifth day Mt. Sumeru was invoked and certain buddhas and bodhisattvas were invited to come into the diagram. The space inside its boundaries was then believed safe from all evil influence. On the seventh day the initiate was given water to drink, symbolizing his thirst for Awakening and his desire to become a buddha. The ritual concluded when the initiate was presented with various objects, including a *vajra*, a gold spatula and a conch symbolizing the sound of the preaching of the doctrine.[2]

The mandala portrays three deities, represented by Sakyamuni, the Lotus, and the Thunderbolt or *vajra*. Two famous eighth century teachers, Amoghavajra (who collected manuscripts in Java) and Subhakarasimhda, disagreed on details of the mandala, including the proper placement of deities. Subhakarasimha argued that the scripture contained false information and mislead those who were not properly initiated.

Some sects of Japanese Buddhism spring from the same sources as Buddhism in ancient Java. Two types of Matrix World mandalas are found in Japan, but Amoghavajra's version is the more common. The Supreme Buddha is called Vairocana and he is surrounded by four buddhas with *mudras* just like those of the statues on the corresponding sides of Borobudur. Jewel or wish-granting vases stand in the four corners. The diagram is bordered with flowers.

Buddhaguhya, another important teacher of the eighth century and the author of an important work called the *Tantrasthavatara*, is recorded to have said that the diagram is analogous to a palace with the flowers corresponding to the palace garden.[3] His remark is interesting in view of the possible connection between Borobudur and the royal family of the Sailendra. We have no proof that temples were important symbols of the ruling elites in Java, but it seems likely that they were. It is also possible that temples were surrounded by beds of flowers that were grown as offerings.

The Diamond World (*Vajradhatu*) Mandala The Diamond World mandala consists of nine small mandalas, of which the central one is called the Diamond World Great Mandala. According to the *Diamond Summit Scripture* this mandala was divided into four parts, each of which contained six mandalas. In each case, the first four represent the emanation of deities by Vairocana, and the last two their reintegration into him.[4]

Vairocana sits at the center of the mandala with four buddhas and 32 bodhisattvas. They are surrounded by 1,000 buddhas and 24 gods who guard the boundaries. As in the Matrix Diagram, many of these are Hindu gods like Siva who would not be converted by reason. A bodhisattva named Vajrapani

had to slay them, then recite a spell to bring them back to life, before they would submit. This diagram also has four gates.

The four buddhas who surround Vairocana include Aksobhya on the east, who makes the gesture of touching the earth; Ratnasambhava on the south, displaying the gesture of charity; Amitabha "Immeasurable Life" on the west, in meditation; and Amoghasiddhi on the north, making a gesture indicating fearlessness. These are the same names used in the Javanese text, *Venerable Greater Vehicle,* and many have concluded that Borobudur's planners denoted the buddha statues on the four lower balustrades by these names. The Diamond World mandala thus emphasizes the number five, symbolized by Buddha, the Thunderbolt, the Jewel, the Lotus, and Karma (Action).

Monumental Mandalas in the Himalayas Mandalas in the form of buildings are rare in East Asia, but are found in Nepal and Tibet. The oldest surviving architectural mandala outside Indonesia was built 200 years after Borobudur at Tabo in Himachal Pradesh, North India. Tabo's central image is a stucco statue of Vairocana with four faces and the *mudra* symbolizing meditation. The temple has frescoes illustrating the life of Buddha and the story of Sudhana, two of the texts found at Borobudur.

Thirty-three statues of deities are placed along the walls in a rectangular arrangement unlike the circular pattern which all texts seem to prescribe. However, a similar system may have existed in Java at the complex of Plaosan, near Prambanan. Some multi-storied buildings in Tibet were designed according to mandala principles. At Sanye, Sakyamuni sits on the ground floor of a five-storied structure; above him are two stories, each of which displays Vairocana, while on the top floor is another deity, Samvara. A building at Tango, Bhutan, has three stories with various buddha images. Another structure built at Gyantse in the fifteenth century has nine levels. The first five represent levels of Mt. Sumeru; Indra's palace in the clouds is represented by the next three stories. At the pinnacle is a stupa.

In Pagan, Burma, many stupas were built on three or five terraces. One of Pagan's most elaborate structures, the Ananda temple, was built around A.D. 1100 to teach the story of Buddha's victory over

Mara. Some 554 glazed ceramic panels on the exterior basement show scenes from the enlightenment: gods parade victoriously across the east side, while Mara and his demons retreat along the west. Eighty panels illustrate scenes from Sakyamuni's life, and 912 panels depict *jatakas*, but some are located where they cannot be seen unless one stands on a ladder, and do not seem to have been meant to form part of the curriculum. Their purpose is unclear.

These architectural mandalas are similar in that they contain rooms. Borobudur is of a very different type—a set of stone terraces with no enclosed space. Examples of this second type are also found in Tibet and Nepal. Numerous Himalayan sanctuaries have five terraces, passageways for ceremonies involving walking around a central stupa, four stairways and statues of five buddhas on the walls. In the Himalayas these are called Dharma World mandalas and are dedicated to Manjusri. Mandalas dedicated to Vairocana are termed Diamond World mandalas.

In Tibet, stupas on stepped plinths cut by four stairways like Borobudur are called "Descent from Heaven" and are only found at sites associated with the sect founded by Atisa, who had spent 20 years in Sumatra. On the other hand, terraced temples were made 5000 years ago in Mesopotamia. One archaeologist suggested that Borobudur's form resulted from the combination of the stupa with the central Asian terraced sanctuary.[5] Although Borobudur's terraced structure is unusual, it is not unique in that respect. Borobudur's special identity lies in the particular structures and motifs set on those terraces.

Closer to Java, temples were built on multi-storied terraces in Cambodia and Champa (south Vietnam). None of these are as old as Borobudur. None combine narrative reliefs, staircases, buddha images, statues, and round stupa terraces in the same manner. Borobudur's complexity is of a much higher order; thus our ability to draw analogies between them and Borobudur is limited.

The mandalas in the Himalayan area are so different from those of Japan that they should perhaps be classified as separate but related concepts. In Nepal, mandalas are divided into Diamond and Dharma World mandalas, while the Japanese distinguish between Diamond and Matrix mandalas.[6] Perhaps different mandala theories coexisted in ancient Java.

APPENDIX C
Thunderbolts

Thunderbolts in Sumatra Seventh-century Srivijayan inscriptions already mention *siddhi* ("success") and supernatural forces obtained by magical methods. In Sumatra, thunderbolts have been found carved on bricks and stone from temples in Riau and North Sumatra, but from sites dated later than Borobudur. One gold plate from a ruined brick structure, perhaps a stupa, at Tanjung Medan, West Sumatra, has an incised four-ended *vajra* surmounted by an eight-petalled lotus in which are written the names of five buddhas, the central place being occupied not by Vairocana, but by Aksobhya. The writing style seems to date from the twelfth century.

Another unusual image is inscribed on a gold plate kept in the Museum Nasional. Its find spot is unknown, but perhaps it is also from Sumatra. This plate is inscribed with a four-ended thunderbolt with a lotus, but the lotus has only two petals. Inside are the names of two buddhas, Ratnasambhava and Amoghasiddhi, with Aksobhya written in the center.

These two plates were probably part of a set of mystical diagrams or *yantra* depicting the levels in the human body according to Yoga Tantra. Yoga practitioners try to awaken a goddess, Devi Kundalini, who sleeps at the base of the backbone, and raise her through six levels of the body to the top of the head. When this occurs, the practitioner feels supreme bliss. The two-petalled lotus symbolizes eye level. It would seem that yogic Buddhism was well-developed in Sumatra in the twelfth century.

The word *bahal*, used to denote brick temples built from the eleventh to thirteenth centuries in Padang Lawas, North Sumatra, is still used in Nepal to refer to Vajrayana temples. These structures have two stories: a lower one for the uninitiated containing statues of the five *jina* buddhas or other images, and a second where the gods of the *vajra* are kept.

Bronze Thunderbolts and Diamond Deities Texts and objects associated with Tantric techniques became increasingly pervasive in Indonesia in the ninth century. One important object used in Tantric rituals is the *vajra* or "thunderbolt." The word *vajra* occurs prominently in the names of many Buddhist missionaries in eighth century Java, including both Vajrabodhi and Amoghavajra, who met in Java in A.D. 718 before proceeding to China to spread the "Way of the Thunderbolt."

Thunderbolts in Java Bronze handbells with thunderbolt handles found in Java sometimes have plain handles.[7] More complex examples have four heads placed between the bell's body and the five prongs of the thunderbolt.[8] Some examples are more complex; one bell made of a bronze-silver alloy in central Java during the late eighth century has five prongs, a blue lotus, and four heads beneath four symbols in relief: a thunderbolt, a jewel, and a red lotus. The fourth symbol has been effaced, but would have been a four-ended thunderbolt. These are symbols of the four buddhas associated with Vairocana.[9]

The most complicated example of such a bell has four heads and eight symbols: four for the buddhas and four for the attendant bodhisattvas.[10] A few such artifacts are also known from east Java.

Bronze statues of Diamond World deities are more common still. Ninety bronze statues were discovered near Nganjuk, East Java, where they had been hidden, probably to preserve them from some danger. They must have belonged to an elaborate three-dimensional mandala. They depict numerous figures who do not appear at Borobudur, but are specified in the Diamond World mandala, such as female bodhisattvas who hold flowers, an incense burner, and a lute. The main image in the group has four faces. According to the *Diamond Summit,* the Supreme Buddha Vairocana has only one face, and he is always shown thus in China and Japan. The *Nispanna-yogavali* describes a four-faced Vairocana and statues in Tibet and Nepal show him in this form.

The bronzes are in a style made two or three centuries after Borobudur. Thus they do not directly enlighten us concerning the use of mandalas in Borobudur's time. In addition to the 90 found at Nganjuk, other examples have been discovered in both central and east Java. Some images depict Vairocana himself, sometimes in the characteristic *bodhyagri mudra*[11] in which the two hands are held in front of the chest, right above left, with the left forefinger held in the palm of the right. A gilt bronze example was discovered at Sidorejo, Central Java.[12] There are also statues of Vairocana's feminine aspect, Vajradatvisvari.

Another Diamond World deity was *Vajrasattva,* "Diamond Being." His statues show him holding a thunderbolt in his right hand, a bell in his left, resting against his hip, with an elephant's head in the base. He personified the buddha consciousness contained in all beings and objects and embodied the 37 "Diamond World Knowledges"; his thunderbolt and bell symbolize these, for they are the signs of the first and last of the 32 bodhisattvas in the Maya mandala, one of eight sub-mandalas of the Diamond World.

Vajrapani ("Diamond Holder") is an important denizen of the Diamond World. One of the most unusual statues ever found in Indonesia depicts Vajrapani in a guise known as Dharmapala. This bronze image, found in Yogyakarta, looks familiar to those acquainted with Tibetan iconography; it shows a violent four-headed, eight-armed god holding a bow, goad, discus, etc, standing on two corpses. These represent Vajrapani's victory over Siva and Uma.

Wrathful gods are rarely depicted in Indonesia, although Old Balinese texts describe deities in this form. Diamond World texts devote much space to describing how enemies of the faith were defeated. In Tibet such wrathful forms became much more influential and popular. In China, Amoghavajra became "Imperial Preceptor" in the eighth century and called upon the aid of Diamond World gods to help conquer living enemies of the kingdom, particularly Tibetans and Arabs. The paired forms of wrathful deities, showing them in sexual intercourse, were popular in Tibet but non-existent in Indonesia. Perhaps the serene and faithful Javanese did not require demonic or lustful deities, for they had already overcome these obstacles to enlightenment.

The Supreme Buddha was symbolized in different forms in various levels of *tantra.* The first level used Amitayus/Amitabha. In the second level, Vairocana (-bhisambodhi) in the meditation pose was used. The third level displayed Vairocana, with four faces and holding the discus, with left forefinger in right fist.

The bronze Diamond World gods and thunderbolts from central Java could all have been made after A.D. 830. But their absence from Borobudur may be due to other causes. Objects were only necessary for people at lower levels of awareness. Perhaps the practices conducted at Borobudur were only meant for people at higher stages of advancement.

NOTES
Part I

1. W.O. Olthof, *Babad Tanah Djawi in Proza* ('s-Gravenhage: M. Nijhoff, 1941), p. 318.

2. J. Brandes, "Twee oude berichten over de Baraboedoer." *Tijdschrift van het Bataviaasch Genootschap* 44 (1901), pp. 73-84.

3. His drawings have been given bad marks for artistic merit as well as for accuracy; J.F. Stutterheim, *De Teekeningen van Javaansche Oudheden in het Rijksmuseum van Ethnografie* (Leiden: Luctor et Emergo, 1933), pp. 50-76.

4. Siddharta is his given name, Gautama his clan.

5. The Sakya are sometimes called a "clan" but this is not correct. A closer equivalent would be "tribe," but this word is imprecise. The Sakya ruler's position was not traditionally inherited; he was chosen from a group of nobles. The story of Siddharta's life suggests that Sakya political organization may have been developing more formal institutions based on hereditary kingship. B. Walker, *Hindu World* (London: Allen and Unwin, 1968), vol. II, p. 340; C. Drekmeier, *Kingship and Community in Early India* (Stanford: Stanford University Press, 1962), pp. 94-95.

6. L. Chandra, "Borobudur as a monument of esoteric Buddhism." *The South East Asian Review* 5/1: 13; I. Snodgrass, *The Matrix and Diamond World Mandalas in Shingon Buddhism* (New Delhi: Sata-Pitaka Series, Indo-Asian Literatures vol. 354, 1988), p. 115

7. L. Chandra, *A Ninth Century Scroll of the Vajradhatu Mandala* (New Delhi: Sata-Pitaka Series, Indo-Asian Literatures vol. 343, 1986), p. 13.

8. A. Wayman, "Reflections on the theory of Barabudur as a mandala," *Barabudur: History and Significance of a Buddhist Monument* (Berkeley Buddhist Studies No. 2, 1982).

9. J.G. de Casparis, *Prasasti Indonesia II* (Bandung: Masa Baru, 1956), pp. 47-167.

10. J.G. de Casparis, "Inscripties uit de Sailendra-tijd." *Prasasti Indonesia* I (Bandung: A.C. Nix, 1950).

11. The golden cast which some reliefs display is not the original color of the stone; it is caused by ochre applied to increase the contrast when the reliefs were being photographed during the Dutch colonial period.

14. F.C. Wilsen, "Boro Boedoer." *Tijdschrift van het Bataviaasch Genootschap voor Kunsten en Wettenschappen* 1 (1852), p. 287.

16. *Notulen van het Bataviaasch Genootschap* 47, (1909), pp. 140-141, 198.

17. *Laporan Tahunan Dinas Purbakala Republic Indonesia 1951-52* (published 1958): photo 32 and p. 14. Gold rings and coins were also discovered near Borobudur in the mid-1800s; *Tijdschrift van het Bataviaasch Genootschap van Kunsten en Wettenschappen* 2, p. VIII; H.C. Millies, *Recherches sur les Monnaies des Indigenes de l'Archipel Indien et de la Peninsule Malaie* (1871), pp. 10-11, plate I nos. 4-5.

18. Photographs of the bronze *vajra*, bell, and statue piece are found in A.J. Bernet Kempers, *Ageless Borobudur* (Wassenaar: Servire, 1976), p. 16, photo 9, and p. 18, photos 13-14.

19. Boechari, "Preliminary report on some archaeological finds around the Borobudur temple." *Pelita Borobudur CC/5, 1976* (published in 1982), pp. 90-95.

Part II

2. According to this theory, the hidden reliefs on the base correspond to Kamadhatu, the "Realm of Desire"; the next four levels with reliefs depicting the lives of the buddhas would represent Rupadhatu, the "Realm of Form," and the round terraces would symbolize Arupadhatu, the "Realm of Formlessness." Most scholars now reject this theory; see e.g. A Wayman, "Reflections on the theory of Barabudur as a mandala," *Barabudur: History and Significance of a Buddhist Monument* (Berkeley Buddhist Studies No. 2, 1982); J.G. de Casparis, "Barabudur," *Encyclopedia of Buddhism*, (Colombo: Government Press, 1968) vol. 2 fasc. 4, ed. by G.P. Malalasekera, cited in L.O. Gomez and H.W. Woodward Jr., "Introduction" to the same volume, p. 10; and L.O. Gomez, "Observations on the role of the *Gandavyuha* in the design of Barabudur" in the same volume, pp. 180-181, and p. 192 n. 32.

3. J. Dumarçay, "Histoire architecturale du Borobudur." *Publications de l'Ecole Française d'Extrême-Orient. Mémoires Archéologiques* 12 (1977).

4. J. Dumarçay, "Les effets perspectifs de l'architecture de l'Asie meridionale", *Publications de l'Ecole Française*

d'Extrême-Orient, Mémoires Archéologiques XV (1983); "Le savoir des maîtres d'oeuvre javanais aux xiiie et xive siecles", Publications de l'Ecole Française d'Extrême-Orient, Mémoires Archéologiques XVII (1986).

5. It is also possible that work was begun in the reign of his successor Samaratunga.

6. J.G. de Casparis, "The dual nature of Barabudur," (Barabudur: History and Significance of a Buddhist Monument (Berkeley Buddhist Studies No. 2 , 1982) p. 69.

7. A.J. Bernet Kempers, Ageless Borobodur (Wassenaar: Servire, 1976), p. 45,47.

8. H. Slusser, Nepal Mandala (Princeton: Princeton University Press, 1982), p. 152.

9. These are often referred to as dhyani buddhas, but most authors agree that the correct term is jina, "conqueror"; J.E. van Lohuizen-de Leeuw, "The Dhyani-Buddhas of Barabudur," Bijdragen tot de Taal-, Land- en Volkenkunde 121 (1965) p.391 note 5.

10. P. Mus, Barabudur (Hanoi: Imprimerie d'Extreme-Orient, 1935), vol. 2, pp. 103 ff.

11. Scripture of the Lotus Blossom of the Fine Dharma, translated by Leon Hurvitz (New York: Columbia University Press, 1976), p. 183.

12. Ibid. p. 178.

13. Ibid. p. 178

14. J.J. Boeles, The Secret of Borobudur (Bangkok: J.J. Boeles, 1985).

16. T. Cleary, Entry into the Realm of Reality (Boston: Shambhala, 1989), vol. 1, p. 141.

Part III

1. The bubble is a common simile in Buddhist philosophy for the impermanent nature of the physical world. According to some accounts, the round body of the stupa also takes its shape from a bubble.

2. This story was also represented twice on other parts of the monument: relief 79 of the lower series of the same balustrade, and reliefs 59-61 of the second balustrade. Why this should have been repeated is unclear, but it has been suggested that the designers used at least three collections of stories in designing the reliefs. The story of the hare was perhaps found in all three.

3. One of the most important works of Borobudur scholarship concentrates on this text; J. Fontein, The Pilgrimage of Sudhana (The Hague: Mouton, 1967). A translation is available: T. Cleary, Entry into the Realm of Reality (Boston: Shambala, 1989). I have used these two sources liberally in writing the following descriptions.

4. Pratyeka means "alone, solitary." Pratyeka buddhas in the "Elder Doctrine" were individuals who attained awakening by themselves, before Sakyamuni revealed the doctrine to all creatures. In Mahayana Buddhism the term had a pejorative sense and denoted selfishness, because after attaining awakening they went directly to Nirvana without helping others. Pratyeka buddhas were contrasted to "Samyah-sami" buddhas who remained in existence to help all beings achieve liberation.

5. N.J. Krom, Archaeological Description of Barabudur (The Hague: Nijhoff, 1927), vol. I. p. 108.

6. For illustrations, see H. Slusser, Nepal Mandala (Princeton: Princeton University Press, 1982), vol. II. Figure 19 shows "Indra-sattal," Khadpur village, a two-story sattal with a square mandala plan; figure 20 depicts "Sundhara-sattal," Patan, which has a rectangular plan.

7. Such pleasure gardens also existed in early Indonesia and one is mentioned in a seventh century inscription from Srivijaya. A Buddhist king had a park built for the benefit of all living creatures in an act meant to acquire merit.

Appendix

1. Sandalwood, aloes, cloves, saffron and camphor. Note that sandalwood, cloves and camphor were special products of ancient Indonesia and the other two could be found there as well.

2. A. Snodgrass, The Matrix and Diamond World Mandalas in Shingon Buddhism (New Delhi: Sata-Pitaka Series, Indo-Asian Literatures Vol. 354, 1988) pp. 155-161.

3. Ibid. p. 554.

4. L. Chandra, A Ninth Century Scroll of the Vajradhatu Mandala (New Delhi: Sata-Pitaka Series, Indo-Asian Literatures, vol. 343, 1986)

5. W.F. Stutterheim, "Chandi Borobudur: Name, Form, Meaning," Studies in Archaeology (The Hague: M. Nijhoff, 1956), p. 35.

6. P. H. Pott, *Yoga and Yantra* (The Hague: M. Nijhoff, 1966), p. 72.

7. J. E. van Lohuizen-de Leeuw, *Indo-Javanese Metalwork* (Stuttgart: Linden-Museum, 1984) pl. 67; Scheurleer and Klokke (1984), pl. 68.

8. van Lohuizen-de Leeuw, pl. 63, 64.

9. Ibid. pl. 61; compare pl. 64; also Scheurleer and Klokke (1988) pl. 67.

10. van Lohuizen-de Leeuw, pl. 64.

11. For example van Lohuizen-de Leeuw; pl. 6, 7, from central Java.

12. J. Fontein, R. Soekmoni, Satyawati Suleiman, *Ancient Indonesian Art* (New York: Asia House, 1971) pl. 148.

BIBLIOGRAPHY

Bernet Kempers, A.J. *Ageless Borobudur* (Wassenaar: Servire, 1976).

Boechari. "Preliminary report on some archaeological finds around the Borobudur temple," *Pelita Borobudur CC/5, 1976* (published 1982): Pp. 90-95.

Boeles, J.J. *The Secret of Borobudur* (Bangkok: J.J. Boeles, 1985).

Brandes, J. "Twee oude berichten over de Baraboedoer," *Tijdschrift van het Bataviaasch Genootschap* 44 (1901): Pp. 73-84.

de Casparis, J.G. *Prasasti Indonesia II* (Bandung: Masa Baru, 1956).

de Casparis, J.G. *Prasasti Indonesia I* "Inscripties uit de Sailendra-tijd," (Bandung: A.C. Nix, 1950).

de Casparis, J.G. "Barabudur," *Encyclopedia of Buddhism* (Colombo: Government Press, 1968).

de Casparis, J.G. "The dual nature of Barabudur," *Barabudur: History and Significance of a Buddhist Monument* (Berkeley Buddhist Studies No. 2 , 1981): Pp. 47-83.

Chandra, L. "Borobudur as a monument of esoteric Buddhism," *South East Asian Review* 5/1: 1-41.

Chandra, L. *A Ninth Century Scroll of the Vajradhatu Mandala* (New Delhi: Sata-Pitaka Series, Indo-Asian Literatures, vol. 343, 1986).

Cleary, T. *Entry into the Realm of Reality.* (Boston: Shambhala, 1989).

Drekmeier, C. *Kingship and Community in Early India* (Stanford: Stanford University Press, 1962).

Dumarçay, J. "Histoire architecturale du Borobudur." *Publications de l'Ecole Française d'Extrême-Orient, Mémoires Archéologiques* XII (1977).

Dumarçay, J. "Les effets perspectifs de l'architecture de l'Asie meridionale," *Publications de l'Ecole Française d'Extrême-Orient, Mémoires Archéologiques* XV (1983).

Dumarçay, J. "Le savoir des maîtres d'oeuvre javanais aux xiiie et xive siecles", *Publications de l'Ecole Française d'Extrême-Orient, Mémoires Archéologiques* XVII (1986).

Fontein, J. *The Pilgrimage of Sudhana* (The Hague: Mouton, 1967).

Fontein, J.; Soekmono, R.; Satyawati Suleiman, *Ancient Indonesian Art* (New York: Asia House, 1971).

Hurvitz, L., trans. *Scripture of the Lotus Blossom of the Fine Dharma* (New York: Columbia University Press, 1976).

Krom, N.J. and Th. van Erp. *Archaeological Description of Barabudur* (The Hague: M. Nijhoff, 1927-1931).

Laporan Tahunan Dinas Purbakala Republic Indonesia 1951-52 (published 1958).

van Lohuizen-de Leeuw, J.E. *Indo-Javanese Metalwork* (Stuttgart: Linden-Museum, 1984).

van Lohuizen-de Leeuw, J.E. "The Dhyani-Buddhas of Barabudur," *Bijdragen tot de Taal-, Land- en Volkenkunde* 121 (1965).

Millies, H.C. *Recherches sur les Monnaies des Indigènes de l'Archipel Indien et de la Péninsule Malaie* (1871).

Mus, P. *Barabudur* (Hanoi: Imprimerie d'Extrême-Orient, 1935).

Notulen van het Bataviaasch Genootschap voor Kunsten en Wetenschappen (1909: vol. 47).

Olthof, W.O. *Babad Tanah Djawi in Proza* ('s-Gravenhage: M. Nijhoff, 1941).

Pott, P.H. *Yoga and Yantra* (The Hague: M. Nijhoff, 1966).

Scheurleer, P.L. and M.J. Klokke. *Ancient Indonesian Bronzes* (Leiden: Brill, 1988).

Slusser, H. *Nepal Mandala* (Princeton: Princeton University Press, 1982).

Snodgrass, A. *The Matrix and Diamond World Mandalas in Shingon Buddhism* (New Delhi: Sata-Pitaka Series, Indo-Asian Literatures vol. 354, 1988).

Stutterheim, J.F. *De Teekeningen van Javaansche Oudheden in het Rijksmuseum van Ethnografie* (Leiden: Luctor et Emergo, 1933).

Stutterheim, W.F. "Chandi Borobudur: Name, Form, Meaning," *Studies in Indonesian Archaeology* (The Hague: M. Nijhoff, 1956).

Walker, B. *Hindu World* (London: Allen and Unwin, 1968).

Wayman, A. "Reflections on the theory of Barabudur as a mandala," *Barabudur: History and Significance of a Buddhist Monument* (Berkeley Buddhist Studies No. 2, 1981): Pp. 139-172.

Wilsen, F.C. "Boro Boedoer," *Tijdschrift van het Bataviaasch Genootschap voor Kunsten en Wetenschappen* 2 (Batavia: 1852), Pp. 235-299.

With, K. *Java* (Hagen: Folkwang, 1920).

INDEX